From My Kitchen to Yours

food, love & other ingredients

Maria Goretti

Om **Books International**

First published in 2016 by

Om Books International

Corporate & Editorial Office
A-12, Sector 64, Noida 201 301
Uttar Pradesh, India
Phone: +91 120 477 4100
Email: editorial@ombooks.com
Website: www.ombooksinternational.com

Sales Office
107, Ansari Road, Darya Ganj, New Delhi 110 002, India
Phone: +91 11 4000 9000, 2326 3363, 2326 5303
Fax: +91 11 2327 8091
Email: sales@ombooks.com
Website: www.ombooks.com

Text copyright © Maria Goretti
Foreword copyright © Jaya Bachchan

Editors: Shoili Sarkar-Seth, Ipshita Mitra

Photographer: Amit Ashar
Design & Layout: Seek Red
Aesthetics: Sambo Parakh
Make-up: Piyu Palkar
Hair: Sulabha Sonavne

Cover credits
Photograph: Amit Ashar
Make-up: Bianca Louzado
Hair: Sunita Nadkar

Introduction photograph (January, Pg 13): Rosalyn Sayswang
Introduction photograph (February, Pg 28): Location courtesy: The Birdsong Café
Kilimanjaro photographs (June, Pg 92-93): Kabir Khan
Introduction photograph (July, Pg 109): Outfits: Payal Singhal
Introduction photograph (September, Pg 141): Juliet Albuquerque
Introduction photograph (November, Pg 173): Raj Albuquerque

© Om Books International 2016

ISBN: 978-93-83202-03-4

Printed in India by Gopsons Papers Ltd

Printed on Glode Ultra White 120 gsm from Galgo Fine Papers.

10 9 8 7 6 5 4 3 2 1

FOR ZEKE, ZENE AND WARSI
ALWAYS....

FROM JAYA BACHCHAN

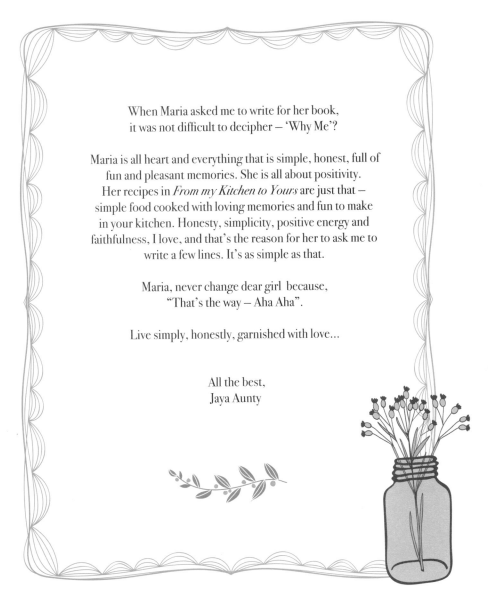

When Maria asked me to write for her book,
it was not difficult to decipher – 'Why Me'?

Maria is all heart and everything that is simple, honest, full of
fun and pleasant memories. She is all about positivity.
Her recipes in *From my Kitchen to Yours* are just that –
simple food cooked with loving memories and fun to make
in your kitchen. Honesty, simplicity, positive energy and
faithfulness, I love, and that's the reason for her to ask me to
write a few lines. It's as simple as that.

Maria, never change dear girl because,
"That's the way – Aha Aha".

Live simply, honestly, garnished with love...

All the best,
Jaya Aunty

Contents

FOREWORD 5

7 INTRODUCTION

JANUARY 10

26 FEBRUARY

MARCH 42

58 APRIL

MAY 74

90 JUNE

JULY 106

122 AUGUST

SEPTEMBER 138

154 OCTOBER

NOVEMBER 170

186 DECEMBER

ACKNOWLEDGEMENTS 202

206 MY TEAM OF INCREDIBLES

SUPPORTING CAST 208

212 GLOSSARY

NOTES 213

About

I have actually loved food all my life. In my past life, I must have been born in a country that had no food, because frankly, I am eternally hungry and my near and dear ones will vouch for that!

My paternal grandma, Agnes, was an awesome cook and if I close my eyes, I can still remember the aromas wafting in from her kitchen; I still remember her picking mushrooms from the garden during the rains to make soup and pâté.

My maternal grandma, Rosemary, was a darling in the kitchen, and her fish curry with rice is something that I would love to have just one more time. Unfortunately, I never learnt any cooking from them because I was just not interested in the whole cooking process. I was very focused on the eating part of it.

My love affair with food started about eight years ago, when I was pregnant with Zene, and had nothing much to do and nowhere to go. Ergo, I spent time watching travel and food shows on TV, and started writing down recipes and trying them out. So while I expanded during my pregnancy, I started experimenting in the kitchen. Fortunately, I was travelling with Arshad for the shooting of a film and was living at the beautiful St. James Apartments. I had plenty of time to saunter through the farmer's market and pick and choose fresh produce, and so I would cook for the cast and crew who came over often. Initially, I wasn't quite sure if they really loved the food or were just being nice; but soon, they began coming over often and looked forward to a tasty meal. I realised then that both my grannies were sprinkling their magic dust on me.

Now, when food is being discussed, my mum's food is what I actually want to learn. I love the food my mum, Joanna, makes. She is my recipe book and is a call away to tell me what to do next if I ever get stuck.

If anyone had told me a few years ago that I would one day put together a food book, I think I would have rolled on the floor laughing. Slogging it out in the kitchen was so not my style. I could eat...and can eat a lot. I have a hearty appetite, despite my tiny frame that, frankly, I do maintain or try to.

After I discovered the joys of cooking, I have not looked back. I started my blog about five years ago, after my domestic help decided to leave. My friend Mini Mathur insisted I watch the film *Julie & Julia* and just would not tell me why; when I did, I suddenly knew my path. Frankly, my help leaving was the best thing that happened to me. Suddenly, I was thrown into the thick of things—the kitchen, the vegetable market, the groceries, the cooking—and to top it all, two very hungry children looking expectantly at me. (I love to picture this scene in my head.) Well! Something had to be cooked, and so I started taking baby steps into the kitchen.

I know myself; I need to get into something deeply if I take it up, or it makes no sense to me at all. Gradually, I started getting seduced by the aromas, textures and the possibilities that could conspire in this beautiful place I discovered in my own home...my kitchen. It was like meeting a stranger and becoming friends. There were so many things I discovered about myself and food that I did not know before. I started reading, googling and watching food like an obsessed person. I discovered the secrets of fire to vegetables, yeast to flour, wine to meat, the right amount of kneading, whipping and marination.

It was like having a lover who gave me so much in return for the quality time I spent that it changed me and my life around. It was then that I realised I love cooking, not just because I could really put myself into the heat of it, but because I loved to see the faces of the people I cooked for. I loved what it did to the ones eating my food.

Jaya Misra, my friend, was the one who introduced me to blogging and insisted that I write about my experience; she always read my pieces before I uploaded them. This whole process of cooking and writing took off, just like being on a surfing board, and I was busy riding wave after wave and enjoying the thrill of cooking, feeding and reaching out to so many like-minded foodies. It was catharsis that I never thought I needed.

At one point, I needed to learn how to make bread, because my dad used to make it when we were kids and by the time I wanted to learn, he said he had forgotten how. So, I joined a one year part-time baking course at Sophia Polytechnic and under the tender hands of Shashi ma'am, I learnt more than I had bargained for. Baking taught me the art of patience, something that I still struggle with. It taught me to respect the fact that everything does happen when it is supposed to happen. Shashi ma'am once caught me staring down at my bread that I had left to prove. And she pointed out that if I kept staring at the dough, it would still not rise up in a second and that it would take its time to prove, so I should concentrate on doing something else during that time. I always think of her when I bake bread now.

I was always hungry for new recipes, new ingredients, and new methods. In the middle of all this, I was anchoring a cooking show and met the lovely Shazmeen, who told me about her stint at Tante Marie. In 2011, I went off to this sleepy town, Woking, and spent 11 weeks at Tante Marie. With amazing teachers, I learnt about sweating onions, kneading puff pastry, cooking meat at just the right temperature to keep it all pink in the middle, understanding how important it was to whip the egg whites till they had the right amount of stiff peaks for a meringue, how to de-bone a fish, how to cut chicken, clean the floors, wash the fridge, do the vessels and much more. In the middle of all this, I also travelled to Paris, Budapest, Austria, Ireland and sat for exams, and watched every play that was worth its salt on the weekends.

The reason all this was possible was because Arshad stayed home and looked after Zeke and Zene; he is quite a rockstar, this chap. My parents too set up tent at my place. And Zoya, Arshad's niece, would ensure that they went for movies and kept them occupied and happy. My friends Mini, Jaya, Sandy and Sambo came in often and took the kids out or just hung with them. I would not have been able to go without this entire web of support that I was lucky enough to have.

My friends in London—Lorraine, Sanjay and Rachna Narang, Junky, Pooja and Eve—were my home away from home. My life is a series of coincidences; I have never ever planned a moment and whatever I did plan never happened. As a kid I never really knew what I was going to do, but I was sure it would be different and exciting. I was willing to work really hard and felt no shame in working; whether it was as a salesgirl in Croissants etc. when I was in college, or being one of the 50 background dancers for a wristwatch commercial. It was all part of a bigger plan that I never knew I was part of. After the commercial, I got my first ad-film, sans a godfather or a professionally done portfolio. I loved dancing and I joined Arshad's troupe. They did plays and ad-films. It wasn't about the money, it filled my soul with unprecedented joy, and that was good enough. He was an awesome choreographer and a fantastic human being.

After years of being part of ad-films, theatre, anchoring TV shows, travelling with work and being an MTV VJ, I was ready for a new chapter in my life. I just wanted to hang my boots, I had had my fill. And having kids had taken over my life and changed it around. Food was just a side-effect of being a mum. This was just the perfect time to put my apron on and go for it, all burners flaming.

Arshad, who was the chef in my kitchen, just took a back seat and sat and watched me, as I struggled my way into food heaven.

He always encouraged me even when the food was really not up to the mark. He always said that it was fantastic and gave me advice on what I should try the next time around. And every time I made *kheema* or *paaya*, he would say, 'It's lovely, but does not taste Muslim!' Well, I really do want to learn cooking Mughlai and Kashmiri food one day and that is on my bucket list. But I did learn to cook, and slowly got into the thick of the woods and spices. And Arshad, who is 'world famous' within our circle of friends for his biryani, bowed out of my kitchen with a smile.

I finally took over my kitchen! For the first time I really started having fun with food. My friend, Mini, started gifting me amazing recipe books and my friends were always willing to eat what I cooked. This really encouraged me, inspite of many disasters too. So post two years of food blogging, I finally got enticed to do a book.

And so now, it's finally here. I remember when the first offer came, I said no, because I was too scared. When the second offer came, I had, by then, digested the fact that probably something is right somewhere, and the third book offer came when I went to the 'Land of Happiness', Bhutan. This trip, that I was never supposed to be on, gifted me one of the most wonderful bunch of friends I had the fortune of meeting. It also finally made me warm up to the idea of doing a food book. Though it did feel like a good idea, it made me nervous; I wasn't a chef, nor was I a writer. I really did not know where to begin. I procrastinated for six months and decided that because I cook only for people whom I love, the book should be an apt reflection of that too. I then started putting menus in place and designing my food according to the people I was cooking for. It was a tedious process writing down recipes and taking care of a teaspoon of this and a tablespoon of that. I never go by accurate measures when I cook for myself. But if I had to give you a recipe that worked, I just had to. I had jumped into the deep end of the pool and had to swim to the shallow.

I could not think of a better photographer for this book other than my friend Amit Ashar. He is someone who will always capture what no one else sees. I still remember the first day of shoot when we were doing the Christmas menu. I brought the baked chicken out of the oven; it was hot, looked yummy, and Amit set up the shot and then looked at me and said, 'Do you have glycerine?' I asked, 'Why?' He explained that food stylists used glycerine to make the food look shiny and moist. I was aghast! Why would anyone do that to good food? So I told him to give me a minute. I took the chicken, warmed up the gravy, poured it over the chicken and we shot the dish. This is how we did the entire book, it is exactly from my kitchen to yours, what you see is what you will get. We never used anything artificial to enhance the look, nothing was overcooked or undercooked to look good. The food was all cooked as per the recipe, and plated up. That's how we started our two years of this book, through the making of a new kitchen, through rain and sunshine, through moving homes, without the use of any artificial light or any glycerine. I just cooked each dish like I was going to serve it to someone I really loved.

Sambo, who was my fashion stylist at MTV, dressed up the table, and checked if the garnish was properly placed, like it was about to make an appearance on screen. Bhavna held the reflector so that the correct amount of sunshine lit up the trees and the shadows were just right. She also collected all the little curios from around my home that we used in most of the frames. We called them our 'able support cast' and they were washed and kept ready before every shoot in case we needed anyone. We were a funny bunch of people working together—a girl who is neither chef nor writer, a photographer who is amazing with human portraits, a reflector holder, who is actually an actor and model, and a first time stylist of aesthetics, who actually styled me for MTV and now styles Arshad for his films.

And we proceeded to have a fantabulous year of food. After every shoot, we devoured everything, and always had a glass of wine or a beer to celebrate. Amit shot this entire book outside my kitchen, on my terrace, in a mix of natural and artificial light. We shot over two years in the middle of children going to school, children and their friends running amok during holidays, house getting repaired, kitchen getting shifted, building a new home, rainy season, no good mangoes in the market, not wanting to cook at all…it was crazy.

We also did a whole lot of celebrations for 'It's done, this is our last shoot', heaved a sigh of relief, and would be at it again, and on our last day of shoot, Amit and I were the only ones present. The last recipe that was shot was the orange cake, that we both ate pieces of and never celebrated the last day of the shoot. It was done, a labour of pure love!

And there is really nothing much I would change about the book. I have kept all the recipes really simple to follow. Just go for it, make it your own, tweak it, have fun with it, and think of me when a smile breaks on the face of the person you have cooked for.

This is me, with all my flavours and enthusiasm, cooked at temperatures that were sometimes too hot to handle and sometimes like a beautiful tropical day, with the freshest of ingredients and cooked with a whole lot of love.

January

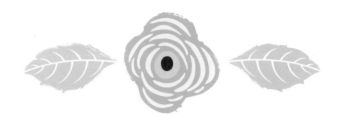

SOUP PALAK SOUP
SALAD BEETROOT SALAD
STARTER RAGI PANCAKE WITH MUSHROOMS
MAIN COURSE (NON-VEGETARIAN) BASA IN
A LIGHT TOMATO GRAVY
MAIN COURSE (VEGETARIAN) YELLOW
PEPPERS STUFFED WITH MIXED VEGETABLES
AND QUINOA
DESSERT PEAR POACHED IN ROSÉ

Salt

While I return from a much indulged year-end holiday, I make New Year resolutions that I most definitely break! I guess we all do. Sometimes I feel they are meant to be broken so that we can come up with a better and more practical alternative.

One such resolution that I have heard, over and over again, is to do with fitness. Many people pledge to hit the gym and have a healthy lifestyle. So, for those very few, who actually start the New Year on that note; this menu is designed and dedicated to you.

If you ask me, I cannot stand diets, they make me unhappy, and that is something I don't like to be. That's why, at the start of every year, no matter what the rest of the resolutions are, whether I make or break them, all I want at the end of the day is to be happy.

And frankly, that's what matters, much like the song from the original soundtrack of Annie, 'You are never fully dressed without a smile.' And I mean a smile that reaches deep within your heart and makes you glow like a little glow-worm, that kind of happiness.

A very wise person once said, 'You are what you eat.'

Well then, I want to eat a 'fit person' to be fit myself! But I am not a cannibal. So, I try and eat healthy and do my regular workout and yoga. And yes, I run. It's one of those things that makes me happy.

This January menu has been designed to make everyone happy. I do not understand starving or not indulging in stuff you like, that is if you can do everything in life with a little bit of common sense, it all works out fine.

So go along with your heart but please take your brain along as well. Eat, love, dance, pray, laugh and hug...and I promise you that you will live a happier and more peaceful life. And never stop eating...but eat well, especially the foods that give you energy to stay bright and happy, with the universe and its collaborators.

CALOROPHYLL
FOR THE BODY

ᔕᴾ Palak Soup

This is a soup my mum made us have as kids. Damn, I hated this! But now that I'm a mum myself, I know the worth
of this soup in gold. And I have it as part of my weekly menu. Of course, I have to say stuff like,
'The Hulk has this', and all the wonderful lies we mums make up, but they are all worth the effort in the big picture.
Also, it's really wonderful if you let the green of the spinach stay a lovely bright colour.
This effectively means that you have not overcooked it so that all the nutrients are not lost.
A 'happy' green makes for a happy you and me!

WHAT YOU NEED

BUTTER - 2 TBSP
GARLIC - 4 CLOVES
ONION - 2 MEDIUM, CUBED
POTATO - 1 MEDIUM-SIZED, PEELED & CUBED
VEGETABLE STOCK - 2 CUPS (1 CUP=237 ML)
TOMATO - 1, CUBED
SPINACH - 250 GM, SHREDDED
MILK - 2 CUPS
SALT - TO TASTE
PEPPER - TO TASTE
NUTMEG - AS GARNISH
CREAM - AS GARNISH

HOW TO MAKE IT

- In a non-stick pan, on medium flame, add the butter.
- Lightly sauté the garlic, add the onions and the potato.
- Add the vegetable stock and boil for about 10-15 minutes or till the potato is cooked.
- Add the tomato and the spinach.
- Let the soup start bubbling; turn off the heat and let the soup cool down.
- When the soup cools down, run the contents through a mixer, and add back to a clean pan on
  medium flame.
- Add the milk and bring to a boil. Let it boil for 3 minutes. Season with salt and pepper.
- Serve hot with nutmeg and a dollop of cream.

Beetroot Salad

I completely love beetroot and have loved it since I was a kid. My mum insisted we eat beetroots. And I think the reason we ate them more was that they made our lips red. Then we would stick our tongues out at each other and make funny faces. So this brings back memories of my childhood. However, this recipe is different; I learnt it from my yoga teacher, Eefa. It is truly addictive and the baked Gruyère is just what brings this recipe together.

WHAT YOU NEED

OLIVE OIL - 2 TBSP
LIME JUICE - 1/2 TSP
BEETROOT - 2, RAW, GRATED
MIXED HEALTH SEEDS - 1/2 TBSP
GRUYÈRE CHEESE - 130 GM

HOW TO MAKE IT

- Whisk the olive oil and lime juice till the mixture is emulsified.
- Pour this emulsion over the grated beetroot and mix with your fingertips.
- Garnish with mixed health seeds.
- Serve with warm Gruyère cheese, which has already been baked at 190°C for 2 minutes.

I LOVE BEETROOT

⒮ᴛ Ragi Pancake with Mushrooms

Now frankly, who on earth wants to eat ragi? Well, I do! And I promise you that you will too, because this is an easy-to-make nutritious snack that looks glamorous as well. You can serve this when you're throwing a party at home. The mushrooms, with that subtle taste of mustard, and the chilli kick are yummy.

WHAT YOU NEED
(RAGI PANCAKES)

RAGI - 1/2 CUP
BAKING SODA - 1/4 TSP
BAKING POWDER - 1/4 TSP
EGG - 1
YOGHURT - 1/2 CUP
SALT - TO TASTE
PEPPER - TO TASTE
VEGETABLE OIL - FOR FRYING

HOW TO MAKE IT

- Mix all the dry ingredients and leave aside for 10 minutes.
- Mix the egg with the yoghurt and add to the dry mix.
- Season with salt and pepper.
- Spray a non-stick heated pan with vegetable oil.
- Spoon out a tablespoon of the batter on the heated pan and cook on either side for about 3-4 minutes or till done.

WHAT YOU NEED
(MUSHROOMS)

VEGETABLE OIL - 1 TBSP
GARLIC - 5-6 CLOVES, FINELY CHOPPED
MUSHROOMS - 100 GM, SLICED
CHILLI FLAKES - 1/4 TSP
MUSTARD - 1 TSP
YOGHURT - 1 TBSP

HOW TO MAKE IT

- In a heated non-stick pan, add the vegetable oil.
- Add the garlic when the oil heats up a little and then add the sliced mushrooms.
- After the mushrooms are cooked and the water released dries up a bit, add the chilli flakes and the mustard. Stir well.
- Take the mixture off the fire and add the yoghurt.
- Add the spread on the surface of the ragi pancakes and serve.

NOW THIS IS WHAT I CALL MAGIC MUSHROOMS !

MY FAVOURITE FOUR LETTER
F-WORD....
.."FISH"....

MNV Basa in a Light Tomato Gravy

This is more like a broth; so you do not really need any rice or bread with this dish. It's tangy and absolutely wholesome. The tomatoes infuse the basa with a subtle flavour and I assure you that the prepared dish will be devoured with great zest. Oh! And if you want, a squeeze of lime will really be nice. You can add a blob of butter too if you like.

WHAT YOU NEED

VEGETABLE OIL - 4 TBSP
GARLIC - 10 CLOVES, WITH SKIN
CHILLI FLAKES - 1 TSP
TOMATOES - 700 GM, CUBED
PUMPKIN - 250 GM, CUBED INTO BIG PIECES
VEGETABLE STOCK - 500 ML
WHITE WINE - 750 ML
PARSLEY - 2 CUPS, LEAVES ONLY
BASA - 4 FILLETS
SALT - TO TASTE
PEPPER - TO TASTE

HOW TO MAKE IT

- In a non-stick pan, on medium flame, heat the oil.
- Add the garlic and chilli flakes one after the other once the oil heats up.
- Add the tomatoes. After 5 minutes, add the pumpkin and cook for 10 minutes.
- Add the vegetable stock and let the mixture boil for about 5 minutes.
- Turn down the heat to medium and cook for an hour or till all vegetables are cooked.
- Add the white wine and the parsley. Let the mixture come to a light simmer.
- Add the basa fillets and cook them in the gravy for 5 minutes.
- Season with salt and pepper.
- Serve hot.

MV Yellow Peppers Stuffed with Mixed Vegetables and Quinoa

I love quinoa; it's a beautiful grain. Have you held raw quinoa in your hands? It's a lovely feeling;
it's tiny but is a robust grain, and is really healthy. I use it in soups, salads and as a full meal.
It's part of my everyday menu and I hope you can make it part of yours too. You won't regret it!
Also, the reason I did not bake the peppers is that they are mildly sweet and crispy, which
infuse so much life into this simple dish.

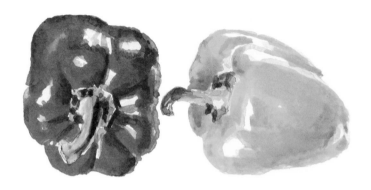

WHAT YOU NEED

QUINOA - 1 CUP, UNCOOKED
OLIVE OIL - 2 TBSP
GARLIC - 4 CLOVES
PEAS - 2 TBSP, BOILED
SALT - TO TASTE
PEPPER - TO TASTE
DILL - 2 TBSP, FINELY CHOPPED
YELLOW PEPPERS - 4, MEDIUM

HOW TO MAKE IT

• Cook the quinoa, drain and keep aside.
• In a non-stick pan, heat the olive oil and add garlic.
• Sauté till the garlic turns brown.
• Add the boiled peas and the quinoa.
• Roast for a bit.
• Season with salt and pepper.
• Add the dill and turn off the heat.
• Add the spread into the prepared empty shells of the yellow peppers.
• Serve hot.

A LITTLE WINE IS GOOD FOR THE SOUL

Pear Poached in Rosé

Frankly, I love eating fruit in its pure form. I'm not the kind who likes to mess with nature and its offerings. Having said that, I do love to poach a pear in wine, sometimes. It has a very decadent feeling to it. The spices, the wine, and the taste of the syrup...they're all so rich and yet not as bad for your waistline.

WHAT YOU NEED

ROSÉ WINE - 2 CUPS
WATER - 3 CUPS
CINNAMON - 1 PIECE
STAR ANISE - 1 PIECE
ORANGE JUICE - 1 CUP, FRESHLY SQUEEZED
PEARS - 4, PEELED
SUGAR - 2 CUP

HOW TO MAKE IT

- Put all the ingredients, except the sugar, in a non-stick vessel and cook on medium flame. Let the mixture come to a light simmer.
- Place the pears carefully in a way that they do not touch each other.
- Poach the pears for about 30 minutes.
- Take the pears out, add the sugar and cook the syrup till halved, or thick enough to coat the back of the spoon.
- Serve the pears with this sauce, warm or chilled.
- Serve with a dollop of ice cream if you are feeling indulgent!

February

LOVE
and
THANKS

SOUP ROAST PUMPKIN SOUP
SALAD AVOCADO WITH SALSA
STARTER ASPARAGUS ROLLS
WITH HOLLANDAISE
MAIN COURSE (NON-VEGETARIAN)
SALMON WITH CRUSTED PISTACHIO
MAIN COURSE (VEGETARIAN)
MUSHROOM RISOTTO
DESSERT STRAWBERRY HEARTS

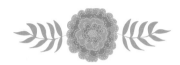

February being the month of love and romance, the menu is dedicated to sweethearts and lovers. But love is so much deeper than just romance and the scope is too vast to be pushed into one day of the year.

Love is what makes the world go round, right? Well, I'm not really sure...because I know that many scientists would completely disagree. But who am I to argue, I'm just someone who loves food at the end of the day.

But I can vouch for myself that love makes my world go round. It's my soul food. I cannot imagine this world without a loving relationship. I love everything about it— the ups and the downs, the highs and the lows, the smiles and the tears, the heartbreaks and the patch-ups. Love to me is as important as the air I breathe in.

Everything I do in life, I try and do with as much love as I can possibly infuse in it.

So what is love?

For me, if you can explain what it is, then it is not love. Because love is hard to define. But more than anything else, it's friendship. To me, love is friendship on fire. There are different types of loving relationships in our life. I think between holding on and letting go, we find a kind of freedom and I guess that is love. It's when you love from the deepest part of your core and are loved back to bits. It's that magical union. It's a place where you know you are safe, loved and protected. It's your mountain and valley of bliss. Life is filled with these moments, and we have been told that expectation is the root cause of all grief and pain in life. So then, what makes us love?

I have never really understood. But like Zeke, my son, says, 'Love is always right.'

Now! Where did he get this information from? He is just 11, but he said that to me, and I just looked at him. How can someone so young, so innocent, who drives me insane with his chatter, say something so profound.

I know that for each one of us, there is one person in this world who will love you more than you can imagine. And you will meet that person as you stroll along life. What happens then? It could last forever or could last for a few fleeting moments. It might change you inside out and bring out your true self.

So live with a heart full of love. Yes, it will get broken, you will cry, but you will live to tell the stories of a moment in time, where you found a piece of your soul that you never knew existed.

With so much talk on 'love', it is just apt to celebrate the feeling with a menu that has been put together to infuse the right amount of naughtiness and romance. The meal doesn't try too hard to be overtly sexy, yet, it has just the right amount of aphrodisiac infused.

At the end of the day, we should make love...not war, right?

IN A MODERN FAIRY TALE,
THE PUMPKIN TURNS
INTO A LOVELY SOUP

Roast Pumpkin Soup

When you're dining with someone you love, not many of you would want to have soup to begin with.
But this is really a fresh one to bet on, and with that tiny kick of vodka, it's fun!
You might not get the taste of vodka, but you will feel it slowly and steadily. Naughty, right?

WHAT YOU NEED

PUMPKIN - 300 GM
OLIVE OIL - 4 TBSP
SALT - TO TASTE
BUTTER - 2 TBSP
STAR ANISE - 1 PIECE
BAY LEAF - 1
ONION - 4, DICED INTO BIG CHUNKS
ALLSPICE - 1/2 TBSP
VEGETABLE STOCK - 4 CUPS
NUTMEG - 1/2 TSP, FRESHLY GRATED
VODKA - 75 ML
BLUE CHEESE - AS GARNISH

HOW TO MAKE IT

- In a baking tray, dice the pumpkin into medium chunks and use 2 tablespoons full of olive oil to drizzle over the chunks so that each one gets coated in oil.
- Add a pinch of salt
- Bake in a pre-heated oven at 180°C for 30 minutes.
- Take out the tray and keep aside.
- In a non-stick pan, on a slightly high flame, add the remaining olive oil.
- Add the butter after a minute.
- Add the star anise and the bay leaf.
- Add the onion and the allspice and sauté for 10 minutes or until brown.
- Add the pumpkin pieces and sauté again on low flame for 15 minutes.
- Add 1½ cup of the stock and let the mix simmer for 25 minutes or until you can mash the pumpkin.
- Let the mix cool down and run through a mixer.
- Add the remaining stock and bring to a boil.
- Add salt and stir in the nutmeg along with the vodka.
- Serve hot with a teaspoon of crumbled blue cheese.

Avocado with Salsa

The first time I ate avocado, I was pregnant with Zene and I had just flown in to NYC from Toronto for a much-needed holiday. I did not even know that I was pregnant till 15 days before I had to leave. My doctor asked me not to travel, but I really wanted to. This was my break; my holiday after two years of 24x7 attention to Zeke. So I went and was in my hotel room all the time in Toronto, and just stepped out for the premier of *Kabul Express*. In NYC, I just spent 15 days of my holiday in bed at my friend Danny and Rani's house. All throughout, the only one meal I went out for was at Dos Caminos where I bit into a guacamole. It was heaven in a bite. After that, when I got back to my bay, I was on a perennial hunt for the perfect avocado, so I could bite into its lusciousness.
This is easily one of my favourite salads in this book. I thought of this because it was part of my celebration feast after I climbed Mt. Kilimanjaro, and they served us avocados as part of our treat. Not only does this dish look beautiful, it's a treat for your taste buds as well.

WHAT YOU NEED

AVOCADO - 4
TOMATO - 1/2, DESEEDED AND DICED
RED PEPPER - 1/4, DICED
LIME - A SQUEEZE
GREEN CHILLI - 1/2, FINELY CHOPPED
BASIL - 4 SPRIGS
FRESH GARLIC - 1 CLOVE, FINELY DICED
CHILLI POWDER - A SPRINKLE
SALT- TO TASTE

HOW TO MAKE IT

- Cut the avocados in half and twist so that the seeds dislodge.
- Mix all the remaining ingredients in a bowl.
- Add the spread into the avocado cup.
- Squeeze some extra lime on the cup and serve fresh.

Asparagus Rolls with Hollandaise

There is something very pretty about stalks of asparagus. To me, they are the vegetable version of lavender stalks, slender and pretty, slightly unassuming, yet, there is something magical about them. The Hollandaise just infuses the right kind of richness to its flavour.

WHAT YOU NEED

(HOLLANDAISE SAUCE)

BUTTER - 1/2 CUP

EGG YOLKS - 4

LEMON JUICE - 1 1/2 TBSP

CAYENNE PEPPER - A PINCH

HOW TO MAKE IT

- Melt the butter on a very low flame.
- Put the egg yolks, lemon juice and cayenne pepper in a blender. Blend till the mixture turns light and fluffy.
- Add the butter to the yolk, one teaspoon at a time, or at a very slow drizzle into the blender till it is incorporated.
- Do not be in a hurry with the last step or your mix will separate and not emulsify properly.

WHAT YOU NEED

(ASPARAGUS ROLLS)

ASPARAGUS SPEARS - 6-8 PIECES

OLIVE OIL - 1 TBSP

BREAD - 6-8 SLICES

BUTTER - 1 TBSP

SESAME SEEDS - AS GARNISH

HOW TO MAKE IT

- Brush each spear of asparagus with olive oil and keep aside.
- Flatten the bread with a rolling pin. Smear each slice with butter.
- Roll the asparagus with the flattened bread.
- Place in a baking tray.
- Sprinkle with sesame seeds.
- Bake at 200°C for 15-20 minutes.
- Garnish and serve with dollops of Hollandaise.

TO SPEAR WITH LOVE

THIS NEEDS THE TEMPERATURE OF LOVE
NOT TOO HOT
NOT TOO COLD

Salmon with Crusted Pistachio

I love salmon. It has a flavour that is distinct and is very tasty.
One thing I keep in mind is not to marinate a salmon with anything strong, but use a very subtle seasoning.
It just brings out its flavour.
So, you need to cook salmon like you would handle a loving relationship. Just the right amount of cuddling and quarrelling.

WHAT YOU NEED

SALMON FILLET - 4 (500 GM IN ALL)
OLIVE OIL - 4 TBSP
FLAT LEAF PARSLEY - 4 TBSP
PISTACHIO - 1/4 CUP
GARLIC - 6 CLOVES, FINELY CHOPPED
BREADCRUMBS - 2 TBSP
MUSTARD - 2 TBSP
SALT - TO TASTE

HOW TO MAKE IT

- Smear the 4 fillets with 2 tablespoons of olive oil and some salt. Leave aside.
- Finely chop the parsley, pistachio and garlic.
- Take a clean bowl and add the previously chopped ingredients to the breadcrumbs.
- Smear the top of each fillet with mustard.
- Press down the parsley mix on to the mustard.
- Bake in a pre-heated oven at 175°C for 12 minutes. (The time could vary depending on the size and thickness of the fillets.)

• • • • • • • • • • • • • •

Mushroom Risotto

There is a certain romance to making a risotto. It's an ideal dish to make if you and your loved one are eating at home because it takes time and patience. And, it's fun cooking together you know. Mundane tasks like washing the rice and dicing the mushrooms are quite fun if you do them with someone you really want to spend time with.

The best part is the wine. This recipe calls for just 100 ml, the rest of the bottle is for the evening ahead.

This is also a perfect dish for romance since you need to keep it on medium flame, stir occasionally and spend time together having a naughty conversation over wine. Frankly, I think nothing is sexier than a beautiful conversation.

For me, the best part of a real relationship is, and will always be, communication. So never let that go.

It's when you share the mundane chores of life that you will see the real face of this splendid thing called 'love.'

So love, to me, is a plate of risotto, made fresh.

HOW TO MAKE IT

- In a non-stick pan, on medium to low flame, add the olive oil and butter.
- Add the garlic and sauté for about a minute.
- Add the onions and cook till translucent.
- Add the Arborio rice and lightly fry for a minute.
- Add a ladle full of heated stock and avoid stirring the rice continuously.
- Let the liquid get absorbed. Continue adding the stock till the rice is cooked and looks creamy. This process will take 30 minutes or cook till the rice is done. (The entire stock need not be added if the rice gets cooked earlier.)
- Add the sliced mushrooms and let them sweat.
- Once the water from the mushrooms starts getting absorbed, add the white wine.
- Cook till the water evaporates.
- Garnish with grated Parmesan cheese.
- Serve hot.

WHAT YOU NEED

OLIVE OIL - 4 TBSP
BUTTER - 2 TBSP
GARLIC - 4 CLOVES
ONIONS - 2, FINELY CHOPPED
ARBORIO RICE - 1 CUP
VEGETABLE STOCK
    OR CHICKEN STOCK - 5 CUPS
MUSHROOMS - 400 GM, SLICED
WHITE WINE - 100 ML
PARMESAN CHEESE - 100 GM, GRATED

- Parmesan -

THIS IS ALWAYS RIGHT

Strawberry Hearts

 D

This is one of the easiest desserts to make. There is something extremely romantic about strawberries. And then when you add to them some sweetened cream cheese, the look and the taste makes gets you into that languorous dreamy kind of zone, in a very cosy kind of way. So, this would be my dessert of choice to end a romantic meal.

WHAT YOU NEED
(TART PASTRY)

FLOUR - 160 GM
SALT - 1 PINCH
BUTTER - 80 GM, CHILLED CUBES
CHILLED WATER - 3-4 TBSP

WHAT YOU NEED
(CREAM FILLING)

CREAM CHEESE - 276 GM
HUNG YOGHURT - 1/4 CUP
SUGAR - 1/2 CUP
VANILLA ESSENCE - 1/2 TSP
CINNAMON POWDER - 1 PINCH
STRAWBERRIES - 1 PACKET, HULLED
        AND CHOPPED INTO BIG PIECES

HOW TO MAKE IT

- Sift the flour and salt in a bowl.
- Add the chilled cubes of butter and cut into them with a pastry knife till they resemble coarse breadcrumbs.
- Use your fingertips to lightly crumble the mixture.
- Add the water and stir with a fork to gather the mixture.
- Gather the pastry into a ball and let it rest in the refrigerator for 20 minutes. (I have used a basic recipe, without egg and sugar. Since the cream cheese filling is very rich, it is all right to keep the crust simple.)
- Roll out the pastry on a smooth floured surface with a thickness of about $\frac{1}{6}^{th}$ of an inch.
- Cut out small circles and make small individual tarts, or else make one big 7-inch tart. You can also just cut out the hearts with a cookie cutter.
- Bake in a pre-heated oven at 180°C, for 5-8 minutes, till slightly brown.
- Let the baked tart hearts cool down. Keep them in an airtight tin and store in a dry place.
- Before serving, mix all the ingredients for the cream cheese filling, except the strawberries, and keep the filling in the refrigerator.
- Serve with a dollop of the prepared cream cheese filling and garnish the tarts with loads of strawberries.

SALAD BAKED FIG SALAD
STARTER ONION IN RED WINE AND
MELBA TOAST
STARTER MANDELI FRY
MAIN COURSE (NON-VEGETARIAN)
LAMB MOILE
MAIN COURSE (VEGETARIAN)
CLUSTER BEANS (GUAR) AND COCONUT
DESSERT COCONUT PANCAKES

GRANDMA AGNES AND GRANDPA CEASER

GRANDMA ROSEMARY AND GRANDPA MICHAEL

MUM DAD

My mum and dad are the best any kid could ask for. They worked hard, prayed harder, and that's why we are so blessed today. We did not have a fancy life and yet it was filled with all that was good and wonderful. We had all that we needed, not what we wanted.

My parents instilled good values, and too many morals for my own good. They always told me to 'treat everyone like I would want to be treated' and 'to do what I want but never to disrespect or hurt my family'.

I never got pocket money and I had to reach home at midnight, no matter what time I went for a party. Gosh! It used to make me so MAD! Today, I thank them for all that they did and continue to do for me. I'm blessed that I have two guardian angels in my life to look after me.

If I can eat 24x7 today and am still hungry, it's because I got that from my dad. And thanks to his amazing genes, I do not put on weight easily! If I can cook today, it's because my mum is a genie in the kitchen. When I think of her in the kitchen I see her tossing spaghetti with vegetables, boiled eggs, cheese, butter and ham into a huge plate that we would devour like a pack of hungry wolves.

We are East-Indians...and no, we are not from Kolkata. We are very much from Mumbai. And so, being East-Indian, and from Mumbai, I spent all my holidays in Vasai, my maternal grandparents' home. The Vasai home was a big beautiful basic home, of brick and cement and a cow-dung floor. My grandpa's fields lay in front of us; the well was to our left along with the tamarind tree. That tree was our bungee, eons before we knew what bungee was.

My mum had seven siblings and my dad had one brother. So I had plenty of cousins and between these two families I had an amazing childhood. We had a big iron swing that creaked when we swung from it or when we lay on it looking at the coconut trees sway in the afternoon sun. Vasai *melas* and *golas* (handmade crushed ice candy) were what holidays were made of, and also my grandma's fish curry and handmade rice breads. My maternal grandma, Rosemary, was a beautiful woman, and my grandpa was a wonderful man, who plucked the tender leaves of the guava tree with which we used to brush our teeth. Bath was at the well and walks were with my grandpa while he watered his fields. Life was simple and happy at its best.

In Mumbai, I had my paternal grandma, Agnes, who was a beautiful tall brown-eyed woman. Her sister, Aunty Carola, was a nun. I have heard stories of their childhood, of the many suitors who wanted their hands in marriage and stories of horses and carts and mango groves, and a Bombay that I saw through their eyes.

My grandma Agnes used to pick mushrooms out in the rainy season and make soup, much before anyone had even heard of mushroom soup in my part of the world. My grandma Rosemary made poha with mutton. Unfortunately, I never did learn food from them. But now, I harass my mum for everything. My dad cooked too, and we loved his food because he always tried out new recipes. My uncle Casho and his wife Jeanette are awesome cooks. So yes, my family has always been amazing with food and recipes. It just took me time to fit in, I guess! And today, when I look back in time, I feel loved and blessed at my life and realise how rich our culture and traditions are.

As a true-blue East-Indian, none of our celebrations, or special occasions, started with a soup. Hence, I have omitted the soup and have given you another starter to relish!

OH FIG!!!

Baked Fig Salad

SL

This is a tasteful and simple salad. The red wine vinegar just blends into the baked fig juices and you get
a salad dressing that, in my humble opinion, is unparalleled. The arugula or rocket leaves are just the perfect foil for
the sweetness of the figs. Arugula has to be one of my favourite salad leaves after baby spinach.
There is something delicious about this lovely bittersweet leaf that is fresh and crisp to bite into.
It's a leaf that just makes any salad taste better, at least for me.
It also tastes good in pastas. Add these leaves to any hot pasta, toss around and enjoy.

WHAT YOU NEED

FIGS - 4
OLIVE OIL - 2 TBSP
RED WINE VINEGAR - 25 ML
ARUGULA OR ROCKET LEAVES - 70 GM
BLUE CHEESE - 25 GM

HOW TO MAKE IT

- Preheat the oven to 200°C.
- Cut the figs into 4 pieces and douse with olive oil on a baking tray.
- Bake in the oven for 10 minutes or till the figs are nice and puffy.
- Take the baked figs out of the tray and keep aside.
- Add the red wine vinegar and 1 tablespoon of olive oil to the same tray and let the mix emulsify on medium flame.
- Take the tray off the fire.
- Add the arugula leaves to the tray and mix them with the hot dressing.
- Transfer the contents into a salad tray and put the baked figs.
- Serve with crumbled blue cheese.

Onions in Red Wine and Melba Toast

ST

I had this for the first time about three years back in London, when I went to learn how to make macaroons. This was the snack I was offered while my macaroons were getting baked in the oven. And I just couldn't stop tucking into the deliciousness of the crispy toast topped with flavoured onions. It's so simple and absolutely yummy that you must try this out.

WHAT YOU NEED

BREAD SLICES - 10, FLATTENED WITH
    A ROLLING PIN
OLIVE OIL - 2 TBSP
BUTTER - 50 GM
ONION - 550 GM, FINELY SLICED
SALT - 1 PINCH
BAY LEAF 1
THYME LEAVES - 1 TSP
MUSCOVADO SUGAR - 50 GM
RED WINE - 50 ML

HOW TO MAKE IT

• Preheat the oven to 170°C.
• Lay the flattened bread slices on an oven-proof baking tray and bake the slices on both sides. This process will take 10-14 minutes in total.
• Cut the edges and give a diagonal shape to these slices. You can also use your hand to break them roughly.
• In a pan, on medium flame, heat the olive oil and the butter.
• Add the onions, a pinch of salt, bay leaf, thyme and Muscovado sugar.
• Keep stirring after intervals of 25 minutes or cook till the onions are nice and soft.
• Add the red wine and cook for about 15-20 minutes or till the liquid is reduced.
• The liquid, once evaporated, leaves a fragrant marmalade of onions that can be cooled and served on the toast.

YOU JUST HAVE TO
HAVE ANOTHER BITE

THIS ALWAYS REMINDS
ME OF MY MUM
IT'S FINGER LICKING GOOD

Mandeli Fry

This recipe is so very simple that I was left wondering if I should put this in the book at all! It's because before I started writing, I always thought cook books had to be fancy, but I know that the most amazing part of life and food is their simplicity and flavour. So please do go to the market, buy fresh fish and try this out. My mum used to make this for us and I remember the first time I made this for my friends, the plates were all wiped clean.

WHAT YOU NEED

MANDELI FISH - 24
TURMERIC - 1/2 TSP
LIME - 2 TBSP
EAST-INDIAN BOTTLE MASALA - 1 TBSP
SALT - TO TASTE

HOW TO MAKE IT

- Clean and cut the fish.
- Mix with salt, turmeric, lime and the East-Indian Bottle Masala.
- Deep fry in vegetable oil till the fish becomes golden and crisp.
- Serve hot.

• • • • • • • • • • • • • •

BASSEIN EAST-INDIAN BOTTLE MASALA RECIPE

BEDAKI CHILLIES - 25 GM
KASHMIRI CHILLIES - 25 GM
TURMERIC - 90 GM
CORIANDER SEEDS - 60 GM
CUMIN SEEDS - 30 GM
SESAME SEEDS - 20 GM
POPPY SEEDS - 20 GM

FENNEL SEEDS - 15 GM
MUSTARD SEEDS - 50 GM
BLACK CUMIN - 5 GM
CLOVES - 8 TO 10 PIECES
CARDAMOM - 5 GM
CINNAMON - 5 GM

- Dry roast the ingredients on low flame.
- Pound or grind into a fine powder.
- Store in a clean airtight container and use the entire batch within 6 months.

MNV Lamb Moile

This is my favourite dish from my mum's cooking, but then I also love her prawn curry, her vindaloo, her potato chops and the list is just endless. But this Moile is awesome. Actually, it should be made with duck. But I just cannot, because when I was a kid, my dad one day bought a duck home, just two days before Easter. This ducky ran around in my garden and we played with it and chased it and it chased us back and pecked us and that was fun. A day before Easter it went missing. Well, while we were busy figuring out Easter eggs and trying to curl our hair, it had become Moile.
I'm not a complete vegetarian and I love my meat, but I have never been able to make Moile with duck ever again.

WHAT YOU NEED

LAMB - 1 1/2 KG ON THE BONE
VEGETABLE OIL - 1 CUP
ONIONS - 6, SLICED
EAST-INDIAN BOTTLE
    MASALA - 2 TBSP
TOMATOES - 300 GM

GINGER - 2 TBSP
GARLIC - 1/2 A BIG BULB
COCONUT MILK - 1 1/2 LT
POTATO - 4, CUBED INTO BIG CHUNKS
EAST-INDIAN VINEGAR
    (SUGARCANE VINEGAR) - 1 TSP
SALT - TO TASTE

HOW TO MAKE IT

- In a non-stick pan, with some oil, sear the lamb on both sides to seal the juices. Do this for about 2 minutes on medium flame to brown it a bit.
- Take the lamb pieces out of the pan and keep it aside.
- In the same pan, add the remaining oil and fry the onions till they are completely translucent or a bit brown. Do this for 15 minutes.
- Add the East-Indian Bottle Masala.
- Add the tomatoes and cook them, stirring continuously for 20 minutes or until the mixture leaves some oil.
- Then add the garlic and ginger that has been roughly pounded.
- Add the lamb, and with it, a litre of coconut milk.
- Add the potatoes and let it simmer for 45 minutes. (If you feel you need to cook the meat in a pressure cooker, now's the time. You shut the cooker and cook it on high, till it whistles, then you lower the flame and let 2 more whistles pass. Turn off the gas; let it cool. Open it after it has cooled down and put it back on the fire to simmer and reduce the gravy some more.)
- One you see that the gravy has visibly reduced. Add 1 teaspoon of the East-Indian vinegar and the remaining coconut milk.
- Adjust salt according to taste and bring to a boil.
- Shut it off and it's ready to devour!

EAST-INDIAN VINEGAR RECIPE

SUGARCANE JUICE - 5 LT

- Take fresh sugarcane juice, without any additives. Keep it in a glass jar or a plastic canister. Keep it undisturbed, for a year, in a cool and dry place.
- The East Indian Vinegar or sugarcane vinegar is then ready. (You can also buy it from a shop that stocks East-Indian masalas.)

THIS DISH ALWAYS TAKES ME BACK TO VASAI

Cluster Beans (Guar) and Coconut

MV

This is one of my favourite preparations of cluster beans. It was made by my mum's sisters for a celebration we call 'Paani' that happens a day before a wedding. This dish is simple and absolutely yummy. I have not been very generous with the oil, but if you want to, it's the East-Indian way to go. And the fresh coconut at the end of it is just the deal clincher!

WHAT YOU NEED

GUAR - 250 GM
OIL - 4 TBSP
ONION - 2, SLICED
CHILLI - 1
GARLIC - 4 CLOVES
TURMERIC - 1/2 TSP
COCONUT - 1/2, FRESHLY SCRAPED
SALT - TO TASTE
PEPPER - TO TASTE

HOW TO MAKE IT

- Wash and cut the guar into ½-inch pieces.
- Boil in slightly salted water for 30 minutes.
- In a non-stick pan, add the oil.
- Add the onions and cook till soft.
- Add the chilli and garlic.
- Add the guar.
- Add turmeric and cook for 5-7 minutes.
- Add the coconut and stir well.
- Season the dish with salt and pepper.
- Serve hot.

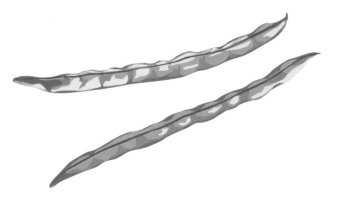

Coconut Pancakes

Well, this is exactly how you make crêpes, but we East-Indians call it pancakes. This is a dessert I have grown up with; the batter is cooked like a thin sheet and then sweet coconut is rolled into it. I love coconut.
It's one of those ingredients I love putting into whatever I cook. And this pancake has just the right amount of sweetness, and is a very simple dessert that I'm sure not too many of you have tasted, unless of course you are East-Indian like me.
My grandma and mum used to make this a lot, which is why it tastes like home.

WHAT YOU NEED
(PANCAKES)

EGG - 1
FLOUR - 1/2 CUP
MILK - 1/4 CUP + 1/3 CUP
WATER - 1/4 CUP
BUTTER - 1 1/2 TBSP +
       EXTRA FOR SMEARING ON THE PAN
SALT - TO TASTE

HOW TO MAKE IT

- Whisk the egg and add flour.
- Add the milk and water, gradually.
- Melt the butter in the microwave and add to the batter.
- Smear the non-stick pan with butter.
- Add ¼ cup of the batter. For the batter to spread evenly, tilt the pan in a circular motion.
- Cook only one side, so that the top stays smooth, for about 2-3 minutes.

WHAT YOU NEED
(FILLING)

GRATED COCONUT - 120 GM
CASTOR SUGAR - 3 TBSP
FOOD COLOUR - A DROP

HOW TO MAKE IT

- Put the grated coconut in a pre-heated pan and cook on medium flame.
- Add the castor sugar and mix well till melted.
- Add the food colour and turn off the heat.
- Let the mix cool down.
- Take a pancake and spread a big spoonful of the prepared coconut mix over it.
- Fold into a roll.
- Serve warm or chilled, either plain or with ice cream.

THIS REMINDS ME OF MY
GRANDMA AGNES AND
HOW LOUD SHE COULD
WHISTLE

April

SOUP POTATO AND LEEK SOUP
SALAD ROASTED PEPPER SALAD
STARTER TOMATO, ONION AND BASIL
BRUSCHETTA
MAIN COURSE (NON-VEGETARIAN)
CLAMS IN A CREAMY WINE SAUCE
MAIN COURSE (VEGETARIAN)
VEGETABLE SOUFFLÉ
DESSERT ORANGE CAKE

IF HE IS EAST, THEN I'M WEST,
IF HE IS NORTH, THEN I'M SOUTH,
AND FOR ALL THAT IT'S WORTH;
WITHOUT ONE, THE OTHER WOULD NEVER KNOW
WHERE IT ACTUALLY WAS.

So, the story started when I saw him for the first time and I thought he was very cute. With long hair and an earring, he danced better than Patrick Swayze.

Yes, I'm talking about Arshad Warsi.

He was everything my mum warned me about. No, it was not love at first sight or anything like that. But I had not met someone like him. Actually, we didn't really meet that day. I met him formally when he came to judge a competition at Malhar, the festival held at St. Xavier's College. I was participating, from St. Andrew's, and our team was doing the tap dance. He had come backstage to give us a few dance tips for the finals and to ask me if I would be interested to dance in his troupe.

Me being me, I said a big 'NO.' We exchanged numbers and that was that.

He then invited me to watch a play he had choreographed. And what I saw on stage blew my mind away. I had not seen someone dance like him in India. Well, he represented India in the World Dance Championship held in London when he

was just 16. He finished fourth on the world stage. And so began my journey into the wonderful crazy world of dance and drama with 'Warsi' (this is the name by which I lovingly address my man).

He was a fantastic choreographer and a wonderful person with a very soft heart. That's why our troupe may not have had the best dancers, because he enveloped anyone and everyone who wanted to dance or needed to do something to earn an extra buck in life. We danced for years, did various plays, stage shows, and ad-films; that's how I got my first ad-film.

And then one day, I fell in love with this mad man full of contradictions. And my life has never been the same. All I can say is that sometimes I feel like I am meeting the lion from the movie *Lion King*, or sometimes, I am meeting Charlie Chaplin. Sometimes I am fighting it out with Bruce Lee; or hanging out with the eccentric artist Salvador Dalí; and sometimes looking at Mel Gibson from What Women Want. In hindsight...had I not met Arshad, I would have had a very boring life.

Two fire signs thrown together may not be a great idea because then, all that happens is that both start a fire and burn everything. Well, we have had many of those, but as you would know, after a forest fire, the land gets really fertile to start anew.

I have no idea what tomorrow may bring, but I have to say a big thank you to the man who believed that I could dance like no one else; who believed that I would be fantastic on MTV; who never reads anything I write, but says he knows it will be good. He lets me make travel plans while watching movies. He thinks I'm an amazing mum, even though at times I have serious doubts about my level of patience. He thinks that I always look pretty and hates make-up on my face. He thinks when the kids behave badly, they are behaving like me, and when they are well-behaved, they are like him. He thinks I'm too hyper for my own good and knows that even though I still cannot make a proper cup of tea, I have that little magic in my food that I should explore. He always lets me be how I am and encourages me to walk on uncharted paths, even if he knows that I may get lost.

The thing is that, even if I do, I always know he is walking 10 steps behind me, so that I feel I'm on my own rare adventure. But, if I get frightened, he is only at an arm's length away.

Thank you Warsi, for being you!

So, this April menu is dedicated to the man who loves his food, as much as he loves his kids and his things in the cupboard!

SP Potato and Leek Soup

This soup is not for someone who is frightened of butter, because at the end of it all, I still do add a blob of butter. When you do make this soup, add a little more butter than I have recommended and go for a run the next day. Run on a path that you have not yet tread on. After all, what is life without a little adventure?

WHAT YOU NEED

LEEK - 250 GM
OLIVE OIL - 3 TBSP
BUTTER - 3 TBSP
GARLIC - 3 CLOVES
ONION - 1 BIG, FINELY SLICED
POTATO - 500 GM, CUBED
VEGETABLE STOCK
    OR CHICKEN STOCK - 4 1/2 CUPS
CREAM - 1/2 CUP
SALT - TO TASTE
PEPPER - TO TASTE
CHIVES - 1 TBSP, FINELY CHOPPED

HOW TO MAKE IT

- Sauté the leek in 1½ tablespoons each of olive oil and butter, on medium flame, for about 5 minutes.
- Add the garlic and sauté for a minute.
- Add the onions and cook for 25 minutes.
- In another pan, sauté the cubed potato in the remaining olive oil and butter.
- Cook for 15 minutes on medium to high flame and let the mixture simmer.
- Add the vegetable stock and cook for 45 minutes.
- Purée the leek, onion and the potato together and sieve.
- Add the cream to the sieved mixture.
- Season with salt and pepper.
- Let the mixture simmer for some time.
- Garnish with chives and serve hot.

SL Roasted Pepper Salad

This salad is lovely as the baked juices of the pepper and the balsamic vinegar emulsify and makes for a very interesting dressing. Yes, it is a bit time consuming. But I can tell you this, some things that don't come easy, are really worth the wait.

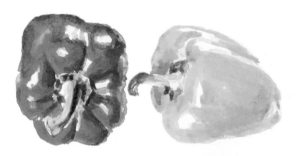

WHAT YOU NEED

RED PEPPER - 2
YELLOW PEPPER - 2
OLIVE OIL - 1 TBSP
LEMON JUICE - 1 TSP
BALSAMIC VINEGAR - 1 TSP

PARSLEY - 1 TBSP, FINELY CHOPPED
SUGAR - 1 TSP
SALT - TO TASTE
OLIVES - 6

HOW TO MAKE IT

- Wash, deseed and cut the peppers into 4 pieces.
- Pour some olive oil and bake in a pre-heated oven at 175°C for 30 minutes.
- Take out the baked peppers and keep them in a covered dish. Allow them to cool down.
- Take the skins out.
- In a separate bowl, add the olive oil, lemon juice and the remaining juices from the peppers, balsamic vinegar, parsley, and sugar.
- Pour the juice mix over the peppers.
- Serve warm or cold.
- Garnish with olives.

FANTASTICO

Tomato, Onion and Basil Bruschetta

ST

Bread always makes everyone happy. It's food for the soul, for any time of the year, be it 'Brun-pao' or 'Gutli.' Basically crusty bread, smeared with our local salted butter, dipped in chai is a taste that never gets out of your system, even though you might taste creamier and tastier butter on your travels. In this dish, the freshness of the tomatoes and the toasted bread, smeared with golden butter, makes for the most satisfying combination.

WHAT YOU NEED

OLIVE OIL - 5
BALSAMIC VINEGAR - 2 TBSP
LEMON JUICE - 1 TBSP
TOMATO - 1/2 KG, CUBED
PARSLEY - 1/4 CUP, CHOPPED
GARLIC - 2 CLOVES, FINELY CHOPPED
LOCAL KADAK PAO OR FRENCH LOAF -
    THICKLY SLICED
PINE NUTS - 2 TBSP, ROASTED, FOR GARNISH

HOW TO MAKE IT

- Emulsify the olive oil, balsamic vinegar and lime juice. Keep aside.
- In another bowl, add the tomato cubes, parsley and garlic.
- Add the oil dressing and toss.
- Place the French bread slices in an oven-proof tray and toast them in a pre-heated oven at 175°C for 5 minutes.
- Smear the butter on the bread slices.
- Spread the tomato mix on the buttered slices and garnish with roasted pine nuts.
- Serve warm and crusty.

MNV Clams in a Creamy Wine Sauce

I love going to the fish market. I just love the buzz, the chatter, the colourful fisher folk and all the amazing gifts from the sea. Fortunately, because I live in Bombay (now Mumbai), I have been introduced to the fish-buying culture from an early age. The men in my family went out and bought fish from the market. I remember going to buy fish with my dad and his brother and they were experts at getting the best deals in the market. I still remember live crabs in my kitchen basin, prawns being cleaned, pink lobsters with beady eyes looking back at us, pomfret, baby shark and my grandma's special clams. She was truly gifted and her food was awesome. Sometimes, when I shut my eyes, I can still hear my grandma and our favourite fisherwoman, Laxmi, haggling. Finally, the fish would be bought, smiles would be exchanged, and the transaction would end on a happy note. Always remember, when you buy clams, they have to be closed, shut tight like a high secret vault, and they must open up when they are cooked, as if you have entered the password to get to the treasure inside.

WHAT YOU NEED

CLAMS - 1 1/2 KG
BUTTER - 2 TBSP
OLIVE OIL - 2 TBSP
GARLIC - 6 CLOVES
SPRING ONIONS - 4, CHOPPED AND
   THE GREEN PART KEPT ASIDE
   TO BE USED LATER
EAST-INDIAN BOTTLE MASALA - 2 TSP
WHITE WINE - 500 ML
CREAM - 200 ML
DILL - 1 BUNCH

HOW TO MAKE IT

- Wash the clams and discard the ones that are open.
- In a heavy-bottomed vessel, on high flame, add the butter and olive oil.
- When heated, add the garlic. Add the onions after 30 seconds.
- Add the East-Indian Bottle Masala once the onions turn translucent and soft.
- Add the white wine after a minute.
- Bring to a slight boil and add the clams. Place a lid on the pan.
- Add the cream after 2 minutes and give the vessel a nice shake. This will make sure that the white wine, cream and clam juices mix well.
- Keep aside for a minute.
- Add the chopped green stalks of the onions and the dill.
- You can have it hot with some kadak pao.

Vegetable Soufflé

MV

This dish is easy, but has to be presented straight from the oven on to the table.
So I suggest you try this when you are cooking for just a small sit-down dinner.
Looking at these beautifully puffed steaming babies is a wonderful sight and the aroma that fills the home is just so wholesome. And don't feel bad if after sometime your soufflé sinks. It's okay but it will still taste too good to be true.

WHAT YOU NEED

RAMEKINS - 6
BUTTER - 50 GM, TO GREASE THE RAMEKINS
PARMESAN CHEESE - 30 GM, FINELY GRATED
WATER - 2 CUPS
SALT - TO TASTE
SPINACH - 1 1/2 CUP, WASHED
VEGETABLE OIL - 3 TBSP
ONION - 1/4 CUP, FINELY DICED OR CHOPPED
GARLIC - 4 CLOVES
CHERRY TOMATO - 6, HALVED
SUNDRIED TOMATO - 2 TBSP
CORN - 3 TBSP

HOW TO MAKE IT

- Butter 6 ramekins and sprinkle the grated Parmesan cheese over them.
- Keep aside in a cool place.
- Boil 2 cups of water with salt.
- Bring the water to a boil and add spinach.
- Lower the flame and let the water simmer for 5 minutes.
- Turn off the heat and drain the water.
- Immerse the spinach in cold water and leave for 15 minutes.
- Strain the water.
- Squeeze excess water from the spinach and keep aside.
- In a non-stick pan, heat the vegetable oil on medium flame.
- Add the onion and cook for 5 minutes or till translucent.
- Stir in the garlic and wait for the aroma to be released.
- Add the cherry tomatoes and cook for 7 minutes or till soft.
- Add the sundried tomatoes and corn.
- Stir well and keep aside to cool down.

WHAT YOU NEED
(WHITE SAUCE)

BUTTER - 1 1/2 TSP
ALL PURPOSE FLOUR - 2 TBSP
MILK - 250 ML
EGG - 3, SEPARATED
SALT - TO TASTE
PEPPER - TO TASTE
CHEDDAR CHEESE - 200 GM

HOW TO MAKE IT

- In a non-stick pan, add the butter.
- Once the butter melts and starts to sizzle, add the flour.
- Let the mixture cook. Stir for 5 minutes.
- Take the mixture off the fire and add a little milk. Keep stirring.
- Put the mixture back on the burner and keep adding milk till you get a thick sauce.
- Allow the sauce to simmer.
- Take the sauce off the burner and add one yolk at a time. Keep stirring.
- Season with salt and pepper. Let the sauce cool down.
- Allow all the cooked items to cool down properly.
- Take a separate bowl and beat the 3 egg whites along with a pinch of salt, till you get steady peaks.
- Add the Cheddar cheese to the white sauce.
- Add the spinach and the mixed vegetable to the white sauce cheese mix.
- Fold in half of the egg whites into the mix very carefully.
- Fold the remaining half thereafter.
- Pour the sauce into the ramekins and bake in a pre-heated oven at 200°C for 14 minutes or till cooked and the tops have turned brown.
- Serve immediately.

Orange Cake

What I learned from Warsi is to never be judgemental. We need to take each other at face value and go from there.
So this gluten-free fresh orange cake is browned on the outside, like a life well lived, and you need to bite into it to discover that
it is just perfectly bitter-sweet and the moist golden yellow inside beams like the sun.
Now that is what I call love and that should stay in your heart.

WHAT YOU NEED

ORANGES - 2 BIG ONES
SUGAR - 225 GM
EGGS - 5
ALMOND FLOUR - 250 GM
FRESH CINNAMON POWDER - 1/2 TSP
BAKING POWDER - 1 TSP
BAKING SODA - 1/2 TSP
CHOCOLATE BUTTONS - A HANDFUL

HOW TO MAKE IT

- Boil the whole oranges, with peel, for 2 hours. Make sure that the oranges are completely immersed in water. Drain the water and leave the oranges to cool down.
- Break into the cooled orange gently and take the pulp out.
- Remove the seeds and discard them.
- Gently scrape the pith of the orange peel.
- In a bowl , blend the orange pulp and peel with the sugar .
- Add 2 full eggs and 3 yolks.
- Add the flour, cinnamon, baking powder and baking soda to this egg batter and mix well.
- In another bowl, beat the 3 egg whites to stiff peaks.
- Fold the egg whites into the cake batter.
- Prepare an 8" tin, and pour half the batter in. Sprinkle with chocolate buttons.
- Add the remaining cake batter.
- Bake in a pre-heated oven with a rotator fan at 170°C for 55 minutes or in a oven without a rotator fan at 190 degress for 40-45 minutes or till a toothpick poked into the middle of the baked cake comes out clean.

SOUP CARROT-TOMATO SOUP
WITH HERB CHEESE BREAD
STARTER LITTLE PIZZETTES
MAIN COURSE (NON VEGETARIAN)
MINI LAMB BURGERS
MAIN COURSE(NON VEGETARIAN)
CHICKEN SAUSAGES
WITH PASTA IN A CHEESY SAUCE
MAIN COURSE (VEGETARIAN)
PASTA IN A CHEESY SAUCE WITH GREEN PEAS
DESSERT ALPHONSO MERINGUE MADNESS

What can I say about them... You want to tear your hair sometimes when they are on a holiday and hovering around you saying, 'Mamma, mamma' every second of the day! And when they are not around...my home is not a home anymore. In my opinion, a house becomes a home with the pitter patter of little feet. I feel that children are the purest part of any relationship.

If I cook today, it's only because of my children. I realised that I needed to make different things so that they do not get bored. So yes, the whole process of cooking began because of Zeke and Zene. It's then that I just fell in love with it. The day they licked their lips and plates clean was a happy day for me. The look on their faces and the empty plates really encouraged me.

The amazing thing about children is that they never really lie. If they do not like it, you know. And they will tell you.

I became the 'master of disguise' and figured how to camouflage the greens (that all children detest) in the most enticing way. I became more health conscious and realised the importance of fitness. And very slowly, my children gave birth to a fitter mum who cooked!

I like children. The more the better, and so I am happy with a houseful of children jumping and yelping. I love the fact that Zeke and Zene's friends love eating at home and that my kids just casually say things like, 'Mamma, make macaroons na' or 'Mamma, please make risotto, but only with Parmesan and no peas, but mushrooms.' I love the fact that they can knead flour and make bread.

I realised that the best way to make children eat is to make them cook. And so I started encouraging them to be part of the cooking process. Whether it's scrubbing and peeling potatoes for a mash, or grating carrots for coleslaw, or mashing up mince to make burger patties, or marinating salmon with olive oil and sea salt, or making momos that even I struggle to get neat; to kneading bread stuffed with cheese and vegetables, they do it. French toast was their first tryst with the cooking process and then there was no looking back.

In fact, Zeke thinks that he is a chef. So, sometimes he rattles recipes to me or what I should do with the next slice of pizza. All this while, Zene has this look on her face that says, 'Silly boy.' One Saturday morning, these two decided to open a restaurant for breakfast. So they took out the previous day's leftovers and made a menu, took down our orders and set the table and served us our food.

Then they insisted we tip them, because they gave us our own line, 'It's good manners.' Zeke now knows his Math, so we can't fool him with coins; Zene is still busy collecting gold coins.

As far as entertaining children goes, I know they love junk. And I think a mix of healthy and junk is good for them. If they do not get it from you, they will jump on it when they do get a chance out. I have never stopped my children from eating or drinking anything except aerated drinks.

Coming back to this May menu, it is ideal for a party at home. Of course, they will look at the soup and say 'Noooo.' But if you say it's 'vampire soup' they may like it! The rest of the menu, including the meringue, is very easy to make with the children and they will really enjoy it.

May for me is the month of holidays and Zene's birthday, so, it's celebration time. So go for it and have a blast!

Carrot-Tomato Soup with Herb Cheese Bread

SP

This soup is simple, delicious, quick to make and nutritious. It can be made at the drop of a hat because the ingredients, I'm sure, are easily available at home. Dad was the 'king' when it came to making all kind of things with flour. When I was growing up, I tried making the Herb Bread quite often, but was never successful. There I learnt patience and the art of making bread. But, this bread is yummy to the point that you will have to stop the children from only eating bread.

WHAT YOU NEED
(CARROT-TOMATO SOUP)

OIL - 2 TBSP
GARLIC - 2 CLOVES
BAY LEAF - 1
ONION - 1, SMALL
TOMATOES - 350 GM
CARROT - 150 GM
POTATO - 1 SMALL
SUGAR - 1 TSP
WATER - 2 1/2 CUPS
BUTTER - 1 TBSP, AS GARNISH
SALT - TO TASTE
PEPPER - TO TASTE

HOW TO MAKE IT

- Heat the oil in a pressure cooker or in a non-stick pan.
- Add the garlic, bay leaf and onions and sauté for a minute.
- Put the remaining ingredients and stir for about 5 minutes.
- Add the water.
- Put the lid on and cook on medium to high flame for 2 whistles.
- Cook for 12-15 minutes on low flame.
- Let the mixture cool down and then blend the contents in a mixer.
- Pour the mixture onto a non-stick pan.
- Bring to a simmer and add a dollop of butter.
- Season with salt and pepper.
- Serve hot with Herb Cheese Bread.

WHAT YOU NEED
(HERB CHEESE BREAD)

GARLIC - 10 CLOVES
ONION - 100 GM
FRESH YEAST - 20 GM
BUTTER - 40 GM, COLD CUBES
FLOUR - 250 GM
EGG - 1
MUSTARD - 1 TSP
MILK - 150 ML
MIXED HERBS - A HANDFUL
CHEDDAR CHEESE - 150 GM

HOW TO MAKE IT

- Preheat the oven to 200°C.
- Sauté the garlic and the onions till the onions turn transparent. Leave aside to cool down.
- Add yeast to a little water and keep aside.
- Add the cold butter cubes to the flour and use your fingertips to crumble till the mix look like breadcrumbs.
- Add the beaten egg and mustard.
- Add the yeast mix and the milk.
- Knead into a smooth non-sticky ball.
- Leave to prove in a warm place for about 35-40 minutes.
- Flatten the proven flour.
- Add the sautéed onions and garlic mixture, herbs and cheese, and knead into the dough.
- Knead into a ball, flatten out and cut into segments.
- Leave to prove for about 30 minutes.
- Brush the proven bread with milk and bake in the oven for 30 minutes.
- Serve with warm soup.

ST Little Pizzettes

I let Zeke knead the dough with Zene supervising the big brother! Zeke thinks that he is this chef who knows everything, and says that all the ideas come to him when he sleeps! Zene has been kneading dough for two years now. So together, they do this with great aplomb. You can choose whatever topping you want, and once you have your choice of toppings, you are in the pizza business. I make a simple sauce with tomatoes, garlic, fresh basil, a little oregano and stock. We roll out the pizzettes into small circles. Some are circles. Some are squares. And some look like...well...never mind! There is nothing more satisfying than biting into a thin crusted, mozzarella dripping, pizza made by the kids and you.

WHAT YOU NEED
(PIZZETTES)

FLOUR - 250 GM

WHEAT FLOUR - A HANDFUL

YEAST - 20 GM

SUGAR - 1/2 TSP

WATER - 150 ML, LUKEWARM

OLIVE OIL - 30 ML

SEMOLINA - 1/2 CUP

TOMATO SAUCE - 1 CUP

MOZZARELLA CHEESE - 500 GM

HOW TO MAKE IT

- Mix both the flours in a bowl.
- In a tiny bowl crumble the yeast, sprinkle with sugar and add 2 tablespoons of water.
- Wait for 5 minutes or till the yeast activates.
- Make a well in the centre of your flour and pour the activated yeast mix into the well.
- Add the remaining water and the olive oil and with a fork mix and bring it all together.
- On a flat clean surface knead the dough for about 10 minutes.
- Place the dough in an oiled bowl and leave to prove for about 40 minutes or till the dough has nearly doubled in size.
- Beat it down again before rolling it out.
- Dust the board with flour and semolina and roll about 16 flat discs on them.
- Garnish with toppings of your choice with fresh mozzarella.
- Bake in the oven for 10-12 minutes each, till the mozzarella bubbles and the pizza dough has turned golden brown and become crisp.

WHAT YOU NEED
(PIZZA SAUCE)

TOMATOES - 4
OLIVE OIL - 2 TBSP
BUTTER - 1 TBSP
GARLIC - 6 CLOVES
ONIONS - 2 MEDIUM, FINELY CHOPPED
CHILLI POWDER - A PINCH
RED PEPPER - 1
CHICKEN STOCK / VEGETABLE STOCK - 100 ML
SALT - TO TASTE
PEPPER - TO TASTE
BASIL LEAVES - A HANDFUL

HOW TO MAKE IT

- Blanch the tomatoes in simmering water for about 5-10 minutes so that the skin is easily peeled off later.
- Take out the tomatoes and immerse in cold water. Keep aside.
- Heat the olive oil and butter.
- Add the finely chopped garlic and sauté for a minute.
- Add the onions and sauté for 10-12 minutes.
- Add the chilli powder.
- Add the chopped bell pepper and cook for 5 minutes.
- Peel the tomatoes, roughly chop them and add them to the pan.
- Sauté for 3-4 minutes.
- Add the stock and cook the mixture on medium flame or till it gets a thick consistency.
- Sprinkle salt and freshly ground pepper.
- Turn off the heat. Add a handful of basil leaves and stir.

"MAMMA, IT'S NOT GOOD
IT'S SIMPLY AWESOME!"
SAID ZEKE AND ZENE

Mini Lamb Burgers

When I was pregnant, all I did was search for the juiciest burgers to devour. No wonder my Zeke and Zene love burgers. The thing about burgers is, you know you've got it right when every bite you take is absolutely juicy and that you just can't stop.

WHAT YOU NEED

LAMB - 500 GM, MINCED
ONION - 1, FINELY CHOPPED + 1, THINLY SLICED &
    PAN-SEARED, FOR GARNISHING
GARLIC - 6, CHOPPED
STALE BREAD SLICES - 4
LIME - 1/2
CHILLI POWDER - 1/2 TSP
PEPPER - 1/2 TSP
SALT - TO TASTE
EGG - 1
BREADCRUMBS - 200 GM, TO COAT THE LAMB PATTIES
BURGER BUNS - 4 TO 6
TOMATO - 1, PAN-SEARED, FOR GARNISHING

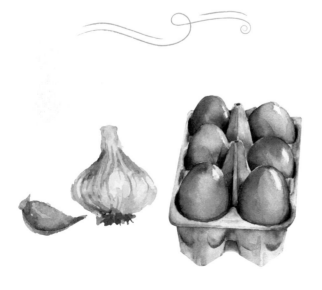

HOW TO MAKE IT

- Mix all the ingredients except the breadcrumbs.
- Let the mixture rest for about 20 minutes.
- Roll out palm-sized flattened discs.
- Press the discs and cover with breadcrumbs.
- In a non-stick pan, fry them in vegetable oil for about 20 minutes each or till cooked.
- Encase in soft buns with tomatoes and onions.

Chicken Sausages with Pasta in a Cheesy Sauce

MNV

According to the in-depth study of my own children, that I have been conducting for the past 11 years of being a 'Mamma', I have come to the conclusion that when everything else fails, pasta and sausages save the day. Always!

WHAT YOU NEED

PASTA - 300 GM
CHICKEN SAUSAGES - 8-10
BUTTER - 3 TBSP
FULL-FAT CREAM- 1 CUP
MASCARPONE CREAM CHEESE - 350 GM
SALT - TO TASTE
PEPPER - TO TASTE
OREGANO - 1 TSP

HOW TO MAKE IT

- Cook the pasta as per package instructions and keep aside.
- Cut the sausages into bite-size pieces.
- Sauté in 1 tablespoon of butter for 5 minutes.

CHEESY SAUCE

- In a non-stick pan, melt the butter.
- Add the full-fat cream and the Mascarpone cream cheese.
- Stir well.
- Season with salt, pepper and oregano.
- Mix the sauce with the pasta and chicken sausages.

Pasta in a Cheesy Sauce with Green Peas

MV

This is a continuation of the previous recipe except that when I feel the need to give my kids a dose of vegetables, this cheesy pasta recipe does the trick.

WHAT YOU NEED

PASTA - 300 GM
BROCCOLI AND PEAS - 225 GM
BUTTER - 1 TBSP
PARMESAN CHEESE - AS GARNISH

Broccoli

HOW TO MAKE IT

- Boil the pasta as per package instructions and keep aside.
- Cut the broccoli florets into bite-size pieces and parboil broccoli in salt water.
- Parboil the peas.
- In a pan, add 2 tablespoons of butter and toss the boiled and drained broccoli pieces and peas. Make sure they get coated with butter.
- Season with salt and pepper.
- Add to the cheesy sauce. (See recipe on page 84).
- Pour the sauce over the prepared pasta.
- Serve hot with some freshly grated Parmesan cheese.

Alphonso Meringue Madness

This is one of the reasons my book took an extra year. The mango season was over and so I waited patiently until the beautiful golden Alphonso visited us again in May to grace our plates.
I make this for Zeke and Zene a lot during May (with mangoes) and during the strawberry season.
They both love meringue and eat it with much relish. This is their favourite dessert.

WHAT YOU NEED
(MERINGUE)

EGG WHITES - 3
SALT - A PINCH
CASTOR SUGAR - 175 GM

HOW TO MAKE IT

- Beat the egg whites with a pinch of salt. Do this with a whisk attached to a bowl. Start whisking slowly for a minute and gradually increase speed for the next 5 minutes.
- Once the egg whites double in size, turn fluffy, and achieve stiff peaks, start adding sugar.
- Add 1 teaspoon of sugar at a time, till the mixture turns into a shiny glossy cloud of white that holds its shape.
- Put the batter into a plastic cone with a thick nozzle.
- Pipe out 6 circles on a baking sheet.
- Bake in the oven at 120°C for 30 minutes; then at 100°C for about 45 minutes.
- Turn the heat off. Without opening the oven, let the contents inside cool.
- Put in an airtight container and store in a cool dry place.

WHAT YOU NEED
(MANGO CREAM)

WHIPPED CREAM - 200 ML
POWDERED SUGAR - 2 TBSP
ALPHONSO MANGOES - 6, DICED

HOW TO MAKE IT

- Whip the cream with 2 tablespoons of powdered sieved sugar and refrigerate.
- Cube the mangoes and refrigerate.
- Pipe the whipped cream on to the meringue.
- Garnish with diced mangoes.
- Serve immediately.

THIS IS MY BARGAINING TOOL
WITH THE KIDS

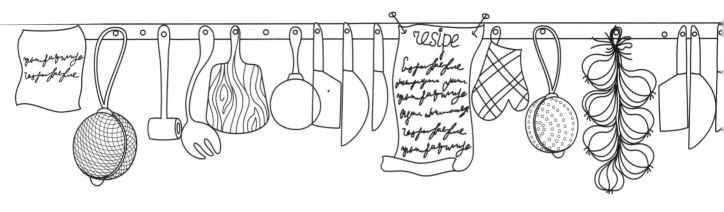

SOUP MIXED VEGETABLE SOUP WITH BARLEY
SALAD POTATO SALAD WITH DILL
STARTER SUN-DRIED TOMATO HUMMUS
MAIN COURSE (NON-VEGETARIAN) CHICKEN
MAPLE SYRUP
MAIN COURSE (VEGETARIAN)
GRILLED ZUCCHINI STUFFED WITH
PASTA ARRABIATA
DESSERT MINT-FLAVOURED BAKED YOGHURT

KILIMANJARO

One day my friend Yudi called me to ask if I would want to be part of an expedition team to Mt. Kilimanjaro to raise awareness about cancer and funds for patients. I was at the vegetable vendor with my mum and dad at that moment and I screamed so loudly that the vendor would have thought I had gone mad. All my parents said was, 'Everybody's looking.' Well, I have never really been bothered with people looking or saying. So, I told my embarrassed parents what I was going to be doing some months down the line.

I was too ecstatic and could not believe it. This was something I had always wanted to do...Mt. Kilimanjaro and the Machu Pichu. I was bursting...and needed to calm myself. I couldn't believe this. Whew!

Now, in retrospect, even my family had undergone the anxiety associated with cancer. A few years ago, my dad was diagnosed with cancer. And we, as a family, kind of never gave in. Since the disease was detected in its initial stage, we were able to get the right medical help. And with a whole lot of positivity and medical aid, my dad is busy living his life like he should, without pain, and in composed dignity. (Except for the regular arguments with me, his eldest, who bullies the hell out of him. Well, that's what daughters do, so I do not feel any guilt!)

What about the thousands who are not fortunate enough to get medical aid? Not able to detect or cure themselves, or the ones they love who are afflicted? What happens to them? Hence, we all climbed Mt. Kilimanjaro to create awareness, raise funds and basically try and help those who are unable to help themselves. I wanted to be a part of this endeavour to overcome my physical and mental constraints and try and summit the tallest free-standing mountain in Africa at 19,440 ft.

And so we all walked: Yudi, Shyamal, Shalu, Tara, Kabir, Anish, Ramshreyas and me. Whether it was pulling one another up, waiting for each other, walking in silence, drinking energy drinks, sharing laughs, warming each other with funny tales on a cold winter night up on this awesome mountain or just trying to sleep well at night in a sleeping bag... We did it all together. We did summit the mighty Mt. Kilimanjaro to greet the beautiful sunrise on October 22, 2012. I think, if nothing else, our determination and will helped us walk through.

And to everyone who has been afflicted by cancer, directly or indirectly, I just want to say we walked for all of you. There is one thing I believe in: we will only understand loss when we lose something we love more than ourselves.

TOO LEGIT

Mixed Vegetable Soup with Barley

SP

This soup is satiating and super healthy. I think if you have a healthy way of life, everything falls into place. And no, you do not have to be a size zero or have abs like Thor! Eat healthy, feel good, make plans, climb mountains, dive into the depths of the deep blue sea. This is healthy for your heart too.

WHAT YOU NEED

CARROT - 2

CELERY - 1

MUSHROOM - 1/3 CUP

ONION - 1

OLIVE OIL - 1 TBSP

GARLIC - 4

THYME - 1/2 TSP

VEGETABLE STOCK - 6 CUPS

BARLEY - 1/2 CUP, SOAKED & DRAINED

PARSLEY - 1/2 CUP

BUTTER - 2 TBSP

SALT - TO TASTE

PEPPER - TO TASTE

HOW TO MAKE IT

- Preheat the oven to 200°C.
- Cube all the vegetables and lay on a baking tray, drizzle with olive oil and bake for 15 minutes.
- Add garlic, thyme and 1 tablespoon of olive oil.
- Stir well.
- Bake for 10 minutes more or till brown.
- Pour a cup of stock into the baking tray and loosen all the vegetables.
- Pour everything into a pan, cook on medium flame and add the barley and 3 cups of stock.
- Cook for 45 minutes or till the barley is cooked.
- Add 2 more cups of stock, parsley and bring to a boil.
- Turn off the burner.
- Stir in the butter.
- Serve hot.

ⓈⓁ Potato Salad with Dill

The amount of carbohydrates our team consumed on the Mt. Kilimanjaro expedition was incredible. What kept me going was the thought, that once I reach the top, there will be hot food on that mountain, somewhere, waiting for us!
It was a lot of fun, climbing that mountain, but it was tough. We all fed off each other's energy to go further.
The sights were beautiful. After sometime we were above the clouds! And it was one of the most beautiful walks of my life.
Our crew and helpers from Nairobi were always singing and smiling. They climbed that majestic beautiful mountain like mountain goats. They skipped, while we sauntered; simple people with smiling faces and shiny eyes.
So this carb-filled salad is in memory of a super climb.

WHAT YOU NEED

BABY POTATOES - 300 GMS
DILL - 20 GM
CAPERS - 1 TBSP
OLIVE OIL - 1 TBSP
BUTTER - 1 TBSP
SPRING ONION - 2, SMALL
RED WINE VINEGAR - 1 TBSP
BLUE CHEESE - 20 GM

HOW TO MAKE IT

- Boil the potatoes for about 25 minutes or till cooked.
- Finely chop the dill and keep aside.
- Coarsely chop the capers.
- In a non-stick pan, on medium flame, add the oil and the butter.
- Add the onions, except the green stalks, and cook till translucent.
- Add the potatoes that are cut in half.
- Now, increase the heat and stir well.
- Put the dill in, stir once and take it off the fire.
- Add the red wine vinegar.
- Garnish with blue cheese.
- Serve immediately.

Sundried Tomato Hummus

ST

Hummus is so full of nutrition and flavour that it is a totally handy snack. Hence, I always keep boiled chickpeas handy in my fridge, in case I have unexpected guests, which I do all the time, thanks to Arshad.

Though it is really easy to make, hummus always gives you the feeling that a lot of effort has gone into making this. If you ever feel you need to adjust the consistency, do it by adding yoghurt and a squeeze of lime.

WHAT YOU NEED

CHICKPEAS - 400 GM
SUNDRIED TOMATOES - 1/2 CUP
TAHINI PASTE - 1/4 CUP
HUNG YOGHURT - 1/2 CUP
GARLIC - 1 CLOVE
LEMON JUICE - 1/4 CUP
OLIVE OIL - 1/4 CUP
SALT - TO TASTE
CAYENNE PEPPER - TO TASTE

HOW TO MAKE IT

- Put all the ingredients in a blender.
- Have it with toasted pita bread or lavash.

MNV Chicken Maple Syrup

'I love cooking with wine, and sometimes, I also put it in my food.'
I read this at a vineyard in Napa Valley and it's something that just stuck in my head.
So, yes, sometimes I do put it in my food, and it just flavours the food so well that it is one of my favourite ingredients.
I read somewhere that men and wine get better with age. I don't want to comment on the men, but chicken marinated in wine for 24 hours is totally yummy.

WHAT YOU NEED

CHICKEN LEGS - 6
RED WINE - 100 ML
MAPLE SYRUP - 2 TBSP
WORCESTERSHIRE SAUCE - 4 TBSP
OLIVE OIL - 2 TBSP
LEMON JUICE - 2 TBSP
GARLIC - 10 CLOVES, NOT PEELED
BLACK PEPPER - 1 TSP
SOYA SAUCE - 1 TBSP
CHILLI FLAKES - 1/2 TBSP
SALT - TO TASTE

HOW TO MAKE IT

- Slice the chicken legs so that the flavour of the marinade seeps in.
- Put all the ingredients in a bowl and whisk it well.
- Pour this onto the chicken and rub the marinade into it.
- Keep in a zip-lock bag and refrigerate overnight.
- Preheat the oven to 190°C.
- Put the chicken on a baking tray and keep it in the centre rack.
- Bake for 25 minutes.
- Serve hot.

Grilled Zucchini Stuffed with Pasta Arrabiata

MV

One day, I was just reminiscing about all the umpteen number of guys I have met and worked with in my entire life. From cinematographers, light men, make-up men, the guys who ironed my clothes, the guy who made sure I was fed, the ones who travelled with me on long journeys so that I felt safe, the ones who I have fainted on at airports, the ones I have dragged to weird places to eat a particular something, the cool handsome men I worked with... Men are lovely and I can say that they are great fun company. And coming back to the Kilimanjaro trip, I looked around at the motley crew of guys that I was on this incredible mountain with... All of them were amazing. So this one is for the boys.

WHAT YOU NEED

ZUCCHINI - 3
OLIVE OIL - 3 TBSP + 1/2 CUP
SPAGHETTI - 350 GM
TOMATOES - 1 KG
ONION - 2, DICED
GARLIC - 8 CLOVES
OREGANO - 1 TSP
CHILLI FLAKES - 1 TSP
SUNDRIED TOMATOES - 2 TBSP
TOMATO PURÉE - 2 TBSP
SUGAR - 1 TBSP
DRY WHITE WINE - 1/2 CUP
BASIL - 1/2 CUP + 1/2 CUP
SALT - TO TASTE
MOZZARELLA CHEESE - 275 GM

HOW TO MAKE IT

- Take 2 zucchinis.
- Slice them into thin strips.
- Smear with olive oil and bake the zucchinis at 190°C for 5 minutes, on either side.
- Keep aside when done.
- Boil the pasta, al dente, and keep aside.
- Bring water to boil.
- Cut the top of the tomato into a cross, skin deep and immerse in boiling water for 5-10 minutes.
- Pour out the water and keep the tomatoes aside to cool down.
- Peel and roughly dice the tomatoes. Keep aside.
- In a non-stick pan, on medium flame, add a little oil.
- In the heated oil, add the onions and sauté for 10 minutes or till translucent.
- Add the garlic and stir well; cook for 5 minutes more.
- Stir in the oregano and add chilli flakes.
- Add the remaining oil and set on high flame.
- When the mixture simmers, add the peeled tomatoes, the sundried tomatoes and the purée.
- Add the sugar and cook on high flame for 5 minutes.
- Add the wine. Allow to simmer on low flame for 15 minutes or till you get a thick sauce.
- Stir in the basil and season with salt.
- Turn off the burner and take out the mixture.
- Mix the al dente spaghetti with the required amount of sauce and stir well.
- On a baking tray, arrange the zucchinis in a cross.
- Take spoonfuls of spaghetti and wrap them in the grilled zucchini.
- Add a loaded tablespoon of mozzarella cheese and a sprig of basil.
- Bake in a pre-heated oven at 190°C for 10-15 minutes or till the mozzarella melts.
- Serve hot with tomato sauce.

Mint-Flavoured Baked Yoghurt

While I was walking down Mt. Kilimanjaro, I was so tired that my mind began wandering... I think I was sleep-walking. I was physically awake and walking for as long as I could remember. I was making up stories in my head to pass time till I found my sleeping bag... Like a day without any plans, where you must indulge yourself, be impulsive and go with the flow. Let your feet lead the way, and in my experience, they take you to where your heart is. So this recipe is, in a way, simple and yet, filled with the right amount of happiness.

WHAT YOU NEED

MILK - 200 ML
FRESH MINT LEAVES - 1 CUP
VANILLA - 1 POD
YOGHURT - 500 GM, STRAINED
CONDENSED MILK - 8 TBSP
RAMEKINS - 6

HOW TO MAKE IT

- Preheat the oven to 110°C.
- In a non-stick vessel, heat the milk with mint and the vanilla pod on medium flame.
- Bring to a boil and let the mixture simmer for 3 minutes.
- Turn off the heat and leave aside to cool down.
- Mix yoghurt with the condensed milk and the cooled strained mint-infused milk.
- Divide the mix into 6 ramekins.
- Put the ramekins into a baking dish filled ¾ with hot water.
- Bake for 15 minutes.
- Cool for at least 2 hours.
- Serve chilled with berries, grated chocolate or relish without any garnish.

THE BEST
THINGS
IN LIFE
ARE SIMPLE

SOUP PAYAA SOUP
SALAD COUSCOUS SALAD
STARTER CHICKEN LIVER ON PAPAD
MAIN COURSE (NON-VEGETARIAN)
SLOW-COOKED LAMB SHANKS
(LAMB KARELI)
MAIN COURSE (VEGETARIAN) MIRCHI
STUFFED WITH PANEER BHURJI
DESSERT KHUBANI KA MEETHA

This month, I present my version of an Eid menu for you. I never ever grew up eating too much of Indian food, being from a Catholic family and the fact that my mum lived most of her grown-up years in Austria.

Dal to me was a luxury; it was the first dish I ever learnt to make because I loved it. I remember waiting for sheer khurma during Eid from my Muslim neighbours and goodies during Diwali. What I do not understand now is that why on earth didn't I try making these dishes before. It's not that food had a religion or any demarcation, or that you were not allowed to cook a particular cuisine in your home. It was only later on in life that I started trying things I liked.

I once came back from a shoot and decided to make cottage cheese with spinach; I was so excited. And it turned out to be palak paneer, something I had never seen before. Arshad had a good laugh then. I remember making the worst sheer khurma one Eid; it all became a big gooey blob. I cried. But the next time, I made the most beautiful well-balanced liquid that was licked off in record time.

I started cooking very late in life and made very few things initially. And I remember every time I cooked, Arshad would say it's very nice, but that I must learn how to make Muslim food. To begin with, no matter what I did, even my payaa and my kheema tasted Catholic, according to

him. And frankly, I just never understood the nuances of this cuisine.

I could never understand how Arshad made biryani; but just whiffing the aroma while he cooked it used to drive me insane. By the way, he makes the best biryani in our circle of family and friends. A mean feat for a man! I think a man who can cook is quite hot. Thank God, for Arshad's sake, I do not know too many who can. Well, I still struggle a bit when I need to make authentic Indian or Muslim food. But today, I can make a mean khichda and liver fry. I have learnt an un-Catholic version of bheja fry as well. Now, I can make a lot of dishes that taste great and most importantly, taste just right for Eid.

But somewhere down the line, I have made my own version of it. I will never ever be able to make kheema or payaa the way Arshad's mum makes. And I'm fine with that. She will always be remembered when I make my version of food, and Arshad will always think of his mum and the amazing food he is never getting. Just like Zeke and Zene will always think that I'm the best cook in the world regardless. And so in this circle of life, don't let anything stop you from trying.

Cook with your whole heart and it will turn out fine. Be a willing student of life and you will know nothing is impossible.

Payaa Soup

The taste and flavour of payaa is something I will never forget as I have had it since I was a kid. I was never very fond of it; it's much later on in life that I kind of warmed up to the thought of having it. The trick is keeping it soupy and cooking it till it gets nice and sticky. The best part is that you can't really overcook it; it only gets softer, but you may dry up all the soup, which is not a great idea. It's best to have it in winter. Serve this warm soup with kadak pao on the side, and the combination is just wholesome.

WHAT YOU NEED

VEGETABLE OIL - 3 TBSP
GREEN CHILLI - 1, DICED
TROTTERS - 8 PIECES
ONION - 1
BAY LEAF - 1
GARLIC - 6 CLOVES
BLACK PEPPER - 8 PEPPERCORNS
MINT LEAVES - 1 HANDFUL
JEERA - 1 TSP
WATER - 5 CUPS
SALT - TO TASTE
FRESH CORIANDER - 1 HANDFUL

HOW TO MAKE IT

- In a pressure cooker, add the oil and heat.
- Add the chilli and immediately turn down the flame to medium.
- Add all the ingredients, except the water and coriander, and sauté for 10-12 minutes.
- Add the water and bring to a slight bubble.
- Put the lid on. On high flame, wait for 5-6 whistles.
- Let the mixture cool down. Remove the lid and add salt into the pressure cooker.
- Put the lid on again and wait for 4 whistles.
- When the pressure reduces, remove the lid and garnish with coriander.
- Serve hot.

SL Couscous Salad

Do you know that couscous actually comes from the northern part of Africa, has travelled all over the world, and is the national dish of Algeria? It intrigues me how food and recipes travel all around the world and how then, different countries lay claim over a tiny grain and bring it to life in their own special way.
There is something very beautiful about this grain; it absorbs flavours and makes itself delicious.
You can use this grain as main meal also, but here, it's in the salad form.

WHAT YOU NEED

CHICKEN STOCK
    OR VEGETABLE STOCK - 1 CUP

COUSCOUS - 1 CUP

OLIVE OIL - 2 TBSP + SOME MORE

LIME JUICE - 2 LIMES

GARLIC - 6 CLOVES

PUMPKIN - 100 GM

PARSLEY - 1 HANDFUL, FINELY CHOPPED

CUCUMBER - 1, DICED

TOMATOES - 1 CUP, DICED

SALT - TO TASTE

HOW TO MAKE IT

- Boil the stock.
- Pour into the bowl of couscous. Add the olive oil and lemon juice.
- Keep the bowl covered.
- In a non-stick pan, add 1 tablespoon of olive oil.
- Sauté the garlic on medium flame till soft and brown.
- Dice the pumpkin into small pieces and smear with olive oil.
- Bake in a pre-heated oven at 190°C for 15 minutes.
- Stir the couscous well, which has been on rest till now, so that the grains are separated.
- Add the parsley, cucumber, tomatoes, garlic and baked pumpkin.
- Season with some salt, if needed and serve.

IT'S TIME TO COUSCOUS

WARSI'S FAVOURITE

ST Chicken Liver on Papad

This recipe belongs to Sheeba, a friend who is an amazing cook and was kind enough to share this one with me. I know a few people who are queasy about organ meat, but will bite into a delicate nibble of pâtés! Well, this is its robust Indian cousin and is an ideal starter. The bite-sized portions are full of flavour and you won't just stop at one.

WHAT YOU NEED

VEGETABLE OIL - 3 TBSP

ONION - 1, FINELY CHOPPED

GINGER-GARLIC PASTE - 2 TBSP

CORIANDER POWDER - 3 TSP

GARAM MASALA - 1 1/2 TSP

BAY LEAF - 1

BLACK PEPPER - 4 PEPPERCORNS

CHICKEN LIVER - 250 GMS

RED CHILLI POWDER - 1 TSP

SAFFRON POWDER - 1 TSP

WATER - 1/2 CUP

YOGHURT - 1 TBSP

FRESH MINT - AS GARNISH

LIME - AS GARNISH

PAPAD - 8-10

HOW TO MAKE IT

- In a non-stick pan, heat some oil on medium flame and sauté the onion, ginger-garlic paste, 1½ teaspoons of coriander powder and garam masala for 10 minutes.
- In another pan, pour 1 tablespoon of oil and let the bay leaf and peppercorns crackle.
- Keep aside to cool down.
- Add the chicken liver to the ginger-garlic paste and onion mix. Sauté for 10 minutes.
- Add the red chilli powder, saffron powder, the remaining coriander powder and cook for another 10 minutes.
- Add ½ a cup of water and cover the lid of the pan and cook till the liver gets tender.
- Add the yoghurt.
- Roughly pound the cooked pepper and add the bay leaf.
- Cook till the water evaporates.
- Garnish with fresh mint and a squeeze of lime.
- Serve on freshly roasted papads.

Slow-Cooked Lamb Shanks (Lamb Kareli)

MNV

Every time Arshad travels, he comes back with a few more names of Indian dishes I have never heard of. He went to Lucknow and could not stop raving about the Kareli he ate there. And so I had to Google, make a few calls and finally try out a few recipes till I was able to get it right. Kareli is a particular 'cut' of the lamb's leg. And you can prepare the dish the way you like. If you are not sure about the tenderness of the meat, please use a pressure cooker. It tastes good when you cook it on an open fire and better still if cooked in an earthen dish. But if all that is not possible, a cooker works fine. This dish is full of flavour and is wholesome too. It is a bit difficult to eat much after this. Unless, of course, the dessert is irresistible.

WHAT YOU NEED

CLOVES - 5

CARDAMOM - 7

GARLIC - 4 TBSP

GINGER - 2 TBSP, JULIENNED

LAMB KARELI - 8 SHANKS

SALT - TO TASTE

HUNG CURD - 5 TBSP

ONION PASTE - MADE FROM 3 ONIONS, SAUTÉED TILL DARK BROWN AND THEN GROUND INTO A PASTE AND KEPT ASIDE

CHILLI POWDER - 1 TSP

STOCK - 4 CUPS

TOMATO - 3, FINELY DICED

GARAM MASALA - 1 TSP

ALMOND PASTE - 4 TSP

SAFFRON - 1/2 TSP

ROSE WATER - 3 DROPS

HOW TO MAKE IT

• Heat the oil in a pan and add the whole spices. Let them crackle.
• Add the garlic and sauté for 3 minutes, then add the ginger.
• Sauté till the ginger and the garlic are brown.
• Add the lamb and a bit of salt.
• Allow the lamb to turn brown. Cook for about 6 minutes on either side.
• Add the hung curd, onion paste and chilli powder.
• Sauté for 8 minutes.
• Add the stock and simmer till the meat is tender.
• If need be, use a pressure cooker and cook on high flame, till the whistle blows. Continue cooking on low flame, and wait for 3 whistles.
• Turn off the heat. Allow standing time.
• Put the cooked lamb into an oven-proof dish.
• Strain the gravy into another pan and add the tomatos and garam masala. Cook till visibly reduced.
• Stir in the almond paste and pour over the lamb.
• Mix the saffron (soaked in a little water) and rose water.
• Seal the dish with dough and simmer for 6 minutes in a pre-heated oven at 190°C.
• Break open the seal and serve hot with phulkas and freshly-cut onions and limes.

THERE ARE VERY
FEW THINGS
ARSHAD WANTS IN LIFE,
BUT THIS HE
INSISTED I LEARN

Mirchi Stuffed with Paneer Bhurji

MV

Paneer, or cottage cheese, is just yummy, even when simply sprinkled with some pepper. And when it is prepared like this, as on the recipe, and stuffed into chillies, you get a new taste. The recipe might seem tedious, but the result is worth every effort.

WHAT YOU NEED

OIL - 1/4 CUP

ONION - 3, CHOPPED

GARLIC - 3 CLOVES, FINELY CHOPPED

GARAM MASALA - 1/2 TSP

CHILLI POWDER - 1 TSP

CORIANDER POWDER - 1/2 TSP

TURMERIC POWDER - 1/2 TSP

TOMATO - 3, CHOPPED

PANEER - 1/2 KG, DICED INTO SMALL
        PIECES OR CRUMBLED

SALT - TO TASTE

BIG GREEN CHILLIES - 8

HOW TO MAKE IT

- In a non-stick pan, on medium flame, add the oil.
- Add the onions to the hot oil.
- Cook for about 10 minutes or till translucent.
- Add the garlic.
- Add all the dry powders after 4 minutes.
- Add the tomatoes after a gap of about 6-7 minutes.
- Cook till the oil separates from the mix. This might take about 15 minutes.
- Add the paneer and stir well.
- Remove the mixture from the fire in 10 minutes and leave aside to cool down.
- Slit the big green chillies lengthwise and deseed them without breaking them.
- Stuff the green chillis with the paneer bhurji.
- Sear on a hot pan or serve raw for that extra crunch.

Khubani ka Meetha

I remember meeting Shaheen in Delhi, with the warmest smile, on a freezing winter day, in January 2000. This is her recipe and she makes this every year when we go to her home to devour a beautifully made Eid meal. It's always a big hit. Eid is celebrated with great gusto at her home, just like Diwali is celebrated at Mini's home and Christmas at my place. It's nice to have friends who make an extended family and are mad foodies too. This dessert is easy, simple to make and so tasty that everyone goes for a second, and sometimes even a third helping. Make sure that you have enough.

WHAT YOU NEED

WATER - 3 CUPS
DRIED APRICOTS - 150 GM
GRANULATED SUGAR - 2 TBSP

HOW TO MAKE IT

- Heat 2 cups of water and bring to a boil.
- Remove from the fire and add the apricots to soak till they are soft and can be deseeded.
- Add 1 cup of water to the deseeded apricot pulp.
- Add the granulated sugar and cook on low flame till the water evaporates and leaves a rich pulp behind. This will take 20 minutes.
- Turn off the heat and keep aside to cool down.
- Refrigerate.

WHAT YOU NEED
(CUSTARD)

MILK - 500 ML
VANILLA CUSTARD POWDER - 2 TBSP
GRANULATED SUGAR - 30 GM
WHIPPED CREAM - 150 ML
SUGAR - TO TASTE

HOW TO MAKE IT

- Add the custard powder to ¼ cup cold milk and dissolve till smooth.
- In a non-stick vessel, heat the remaining milk, till about to simmer.
- Add the dissolved custard mix.
- Keep stirring it continuously. Let the mix simmer and thicken.
- Turn off the heat.
- Keep the mixture aside to cool down and refrigerate.
- Beat the whipped cream with sugar and refrigerate.
- Layer the apricot pulp with the custard and the fresh cream.
- Garnish with apricot almonds.
- Serve chilled.

" O MY GOD!!!
YOU MADE KHUBANI KA MEETHA
LOOK CATHOLIC. HA... HA... HA... "
- SAID ARSHAD

August

SOUP GRILLED TOMATO,
MUSHROOM, BABY CORN CLEAR SOUP
SALAD WATERMELON AND FETA SALAD
STARTER KHAARI, MOZZARELLA
AND CARAMELISED ONION
MAIN COURSE (NON-VEGETARIAN)
LAMB SHANK IN VINDALOO PASTE
MAIN COURSE (VEGETARIAN)
STACK OF AUBERGINE
WITH YOGHURT AND BASIL
DESSERT BRUSCHETTA WITH
CHOCOLATE AND SALT

We all remember our childhood in bits and pieces, and sometimes, we do recollect each and everything that happened during that time. And and an essential part of it are our best friends; who we played with, went to school with or spoke to non-stop. Every girl has a best friend, there are really no two ways about it. And so my life is full of girlfriends, and boys on the side. I can't imagine it any other way!

Ok, so what does friendship mean to me?... Frankly, I don't really know. There may be as many definitions as there are number of people on this earth! Well, for me, friendship is:
An unseen bond which keeps us connected to one another, regardless...
A madness that makes us gravitate towards each other...
Neediness...
A longing to belong...
A need to nurture...
A comfort zone...
Hero worship...
The need for disciples...
The feeling of comfort and warmth...
Maybe, it is the opposite of what we expect and like...
Or then, friendship is like-mindedness...

I'm pretty sure each one of us has at least one friend, if not a whole bunch of them...
We all have different kind of friends...
Friends who will always stand by you no matter what...
Friends who will love you regardless of all your stupidities...
Friends who are always willing to gossip with you...
The ones who gym with you...
The ones who are your running buddies...
School-mom friends...
Yoga friends...
The ones who will always share a bottle of wine with you...
The one who carries you home...
The one who keeps all your secrets...
The one who spills your secrets...
The one whose shoulder you cry on...
The one who mothers you...
The one who sucks your blood like a parasite...
The one you want to slap but do not...
The one you cannot ever imagine life without...
The one you call at 4 a.m....
The one who calls you at 4 a.m....
The one who tells you that the guy you like is an idiot from hell...

The one you want to seriously beat up, because she only makes a beeline for asses from Mars...
The one whose shoulder you cry on when someone breaks your heart...
The one you lend your shoulder to, because someone broke her heart....
The one who is ever ready to shop when sales hit the stores...
The one you want to hit because you have to drag her away screaming from stores...
The one you visit museums with and talk about art...
The one you sit with and abuse guys after a heart to heart...
The ones you get drunk with and then talk rubbish, that everyone, but you, remembers...
The one that looks at you after you are all dressed up and tells you that you look like Cinders...
The one who gives you kaajal to reapply after you have smeared your face with tears...
The one who takes photographs of you fast asleep after putting feathers in your ears...
The one you will fight for till the end of the world...
The one you will let go off, because you feel, she doesn't want to be your friend anymore...
The one you will always take for granted...
The one you will bribe with muffins and sweet things.
The one who will always stay in your heart...forever
I could go on and on...

The fact is, my life is incomplete without my bevy of beautiful pirates...
We plunder, loot and grab life, and make the most of it...
We draw swords and go on wars...
With all who would mess with us...
But at the end of the day, laugh around a table and break bread together...
I know one thing, there is nothing better than a bevy of beauties, who love one another...
Amen.

To all the girls who have touched my life, whether we are still in touch or not, I'm richer that you walked with me for a bit.

Grilled Tomato, Mushroom, Baby Corn Clear Soup

Everytime I cook for my girlfriends, I try and make food that is pretty to look at and healthy to eat.

WHAT YOU NEED

BUTTER - 4 TBSP
OLIVE OIL - 2 TBSP
OREGANO - 1 TBSP
SALT - TO TASTE
CHERRY TOMATOES - 10
BUTTON MUSHROOMS - 12
BABY CORN - 10
CHICKEN STOCK - 4 CUPS

HOW TO MAKE IT

- In a non-stick pan, melt 1 tablespoon of butter with 1 tablespoon of olive oil.
- Mix oregano and some salt.
- Put all the vegetables and set on high flame.
- Let all the vegetables sizzle; the mushrooms will take about 10 minutes to cook.
- Add the chicken stock to the vegetables and bring to a boil.
- Turn off the heat.
- Stir in the remaining butter.
- Serve hot.

Watermelon and Feta Salad

SL

This is exactly the kind of non-fussy salad you want to serve when you are cooking for your girlfriends.
Ironically, my maverick friend Amit Ashar, once came home with a watermelon saying he is going to make something, and we
both proceeded in making and devouring the entire watermelon with feta and mint thrown in.
It's fresh, juicy, and has the right balance of saltiness. The little kick of vodka with the watermelon juice adds to the fun. Please
feel free and add a few teaspoons more, I would not mind that at all.

WHAT YOU NEED

WATERMELON - 1/2
VODKA - 2 TBSP
MINT - A HANDFUL
FETA CHEESE - 1/2 CUP

HOW TO MAKE IT

- Refrigerate the melon till it is chilled.
- Scoop the melon out and keep aside.
- Pour the remaining juice in a separate bowl and add the vodka to it.
- Place the scooped watermelon back into the shell.
- Sprinkle with mint and feta cheese.
- Pour the vodka-infused watermelon juice over the scooped melon.
- Serve chilled.

HI SALAD !

ST Khaari, Mozzarella, and Caramelised Onion

This has just got to be one of the nicest starters to eat if you are adept at making puff pastry. If not, then get yourself a packet of readymade khaari from the bakery and you are in business. And no, you can't be counting carbs today.

WHAT YOU NEED

OLIVE OIL - 1 TBSP
ONION - 2, FINELY SLICED
BALSAMIC VINEGAR - 2 TBSP
KHAARI BISCUIT OR PUFF PASTRY - 10
FRESH MOZZARELLA CHEESE - 150 GM

HOW TO MAKE IT

- In a pan, on medium flame, add the olive oil.
- Add the onions and cook till translucent.
- Add the balsamic vinegar and stir well.
- Turn off the heat.
- Preheat the oven to 190°C.
- Take the khaari, place a piece of fresh mozzarella cheese and add the onions.
- Bake for 5 minutes.
- Serve hot.

Lamb Shank in Vindaloo Paste

MNV

This is a marinade I have grown up tasting and it is something that is a part of me. It's my happy marinade, that I make whenever I want to infuse more happiness into my cooking. You can add it to any kind of meat and in a smaller dose to mixed vegetables as well. This dish reminds me of all my girlfriends; bright, tangy, a bit fiery and full of zing.

WHAT YOU NEED
(VINDALOO PASTE)

KASHMIRI CHILLIES - 100 GM
GINGER - THUMB-SIZE PIECE, CHOPPED
GARLIC - 25 CLOVES, CHOPPED
CUMIN SEEDS - 2 TBSP, ROASTED
EAST-INDIAN VINEGAR - 3 TBSP

HOW TO MAKE IT

• Clean the Kashmiri chillies by taking the stalks out. Remove the seeds from the chillies if you don't like it spicy.
• Add the ginger, garlic and the roasted cumin seeds.
• See East-Indian Vinegar recipe on page 52.
• Grind everything into a paste while adding the vinegar, 1 tablespoon at a time, till it turns thick.

WHAT YOU NEED
(LAMB SHANKS)

VINDALOO PASTE - 6 TBSP
LAMB RIBS - 1 DOZEN
VEGETABLE OIL - 6 TBSP
WATER - 1/2 CUP
SALT - TO TASTE

HOW TO MAKE IT

• Marinate the lamb with the Vindaloo paste and leave overnight.
• Heat the oil in a pressure cooker.
• Add the marinated meat and sauté for about a minute.
• Add the water and put the lid on.
• After 2 whistles on high flame, allow the contents to stand on low flame for 15 minutes.
• Turn off the gas.
• Once the contents cool down, open the cooker and check. If there is too much water, let it dry up a bit on medium flame.
• Serve fresh with bread.

THIS IS ALWAYS EATEN IN SIN-DROP SILENCE

Stack of Aubergine with Yoghurt and Basil

MV

Aubergine always reminds me of home. This is one vegetable I completely love. My mum was forced to make me fried aubergine nearly every day of my school life because I loved to eat it, sandwiched between two breads. Even today, grilled or pan-fried aubergine, tossed in a salad, hits the right note with me. The first time I ate aubergine with yoghurt was at my friend Mini's house. And I just fell in love with it. Finally, when I got interested in cooking, she taught me how to make it. Her recipe, with a little add-on, is now part of my home, just like she will always be.

WHAT YOU NEED

AUBERGINE - 150 GM, SLICED
SALT - TO TASTE
OLIVE OIL - 5 TBSP
GARLIC - 10 CLOVES
BASIL - 8 FRESH LEAVES
DRIED RED CHILLI - 2
HUNG YOGHURT - 500 GM
CUMIN - 1 TSP, ROASTED & POWDERED
SUGAR - 1 TSP, POWDERED
PINE NUTS - 2 TBSP, ROASTED

HOW TO MAKE IT

- Slice the aubergine along the breadth into ½-inch slices.
- Sprinkle a little salt and leave aside for 40 minutes.
- In a pan, add 3 tablespoons of oil and fry each piece on either side for 9 minutes. Leave aside to cool down.
- Clean and finely chop the garlic.
- Sauté in 1 tablespoon of oil.
- Add the basil and turn off the heat. Leave aside.
- Fry the red chillies in the remaining oil and then drain them of all the oil.
- Whip the hung yoghurt with the roasted cumin and 2 teaspoons of the garlic-basil mix and sugar.
- Prepare a layer of aubergine, spread the yoghurt and sprinkle some garlic.
- Prepare two layers or about 6-8 individual stacks.
- Garnish with pine nuts.

135

Bruschetta with Chocolate and Salt

There is nothing better at the end of a lovely brunch than a whole lot of beautiful girls in a kitchen cutting bread and melting chocolate. Sounds lovely, right? This dish can be rustled up in minutes, when everyone else is finishing their meal. It's uncomplicated just like my girlfriends. Just kidding!

WHAT YOU NEED
(DULCE DE LECHE)

CONDENSED MILK - 1 CAN
WATER

HOW TO MAKE IT

- Make 2 holes in the lid of the can of condensed milk.
- Immerse the can ¾ in a vessel of water.
- Bring the water to a boil, on medium flame, and let it simmer for 2 and ½ hours.
- Keep adding hot water if the level of the water decreases.
- Allow the water to cool down.
- Transfer all the contents to a clean dry container.

WHAT YOU NEED
(BRUSCHETTA WITH CHOCOLATE AND SALT)

BAGUETTE - 1
BUTTER - 40 GM
DULCE DE LECHE - 100 GM
COOKING CHOCOLATE - 100 GM
CHILLI FLAKES - 1/4 TSP
SEA SALT - A SPRINKLE

HOW TO MAKE IT

- Cut the baguette into 10 slices, about ¼-inch thick.
- Smear with butter.
- Bake in a pre-heated oven at 175°C for 5 minutes.
- Take out the slices and smear with the dulce de leche and pile each piece with chocolate.
- Bake for another 5-7 minutes at 175°C.
- Take out the slices and sprinkle with chilli flakes and a little sea salt.
- Serve immediately.

September

SOUP FRENCH ONION SOUP
SALAD KALE SALAD
STARTER CHEESY POTATO SKINS
MAIN COURSE (NON-VEGETARIAN) CHICKEN BREAST
IN COCONUT CREAM
MAIN COURSE (VEGETARIAN) CAULIFLOWER GRATIN
DESSERT LEMON TART WITH MERINGUE

On September 26, 2010, I left for my Cordon Bleu certificate course to Tante Marie in the UK. When I boarded my flight for London, I was very apprehensive, yet excited. While I was going, Arshad sent me an audio message, 'It's okay if it does not work out; just come back.' I told him, 'I will finish this work and do it really well.'

I had never really lived alone. In fact, never! So this was actually going to be a growing up experience. Luckily for me, I walked into the home of Eve, my landlady in Woking. I preferred a home-stay as I was more comfortable in a house with someone in it. I had my college friend Lorraine also in London. Then there was Rachna and Sanjay, who were just wonderful to hang around with. Vinod and Pooja were in Budapest, whose house I went to at a time when I needed a home to just sink into. I felt so blessed having all of them around.

These 11 weeks, staying on my own, changed something in my DNA. There was a shift in my perception about life, love and other ingredients. It was just me for the first time in life; I had to only look after me. It took me some time to get used to this fact. But when it finally sank in, it released endorphins for a lifetime. I found myself. I found joy in the little things in life like the smell of fresh herbs, the burnt crust of bread, the smoothness of whipped cream, the perfect crispness of a French fry, and the perfect nap time of 35 minutes from Woking to Waterloo. I jumped in and out of trains like I had a map running through my veins. I travelled to Paris, Budapest, Ireland. I went for vampire movies alone. And walked back with a hot chocolate to scare away the fright. I had the best landlady ever and the sweetest room with a terrace.

School was exactly five minutes away and it was such a fun place to go to. My instructors, Ally, Al, Nick, Vera, Kate and Tim were awesome, fun, super with their techniques and their volume of knowledge about the art of cooking. But I hated exams. It did me in. I served a baked chicken that never got baked! I crumbled outside my school lane. I cried like I hadn't in a very long time, loudly, and not bothered about being heard. I thought this was the end.

But it was just a new beginning, one that taught me not to be too sure of myself; a beginning that made me realise that with food, I'm going to be a student for life. And that's exactly how I love it. I'm always going to cook...with all my heart, and if it does not turn out like I imagined, then I will cry my heart out. But this will not stop me from walking those 10 miles all over again.

I loved what I learnt in my 11 weeks in Tante Marie. It taught me that I need to have patience and not give up. And if something does go wrong, well...it's not the end of the world.

THIS IS AS MUCH FRENCH
AS I CAN SPEAK

French Onion Soup

Another adventure happened during this trip when I decided I would take a train to Paris. During our lunch break one day, I suddenly said that I was going to Paris and asked if anyone would like to join me. My colleague, Mya, from Korea, was the only one to jump at the prospect. The Friday, after the school ended, Mya met me at the tube station, all ready to go off to Paris by the Eurostar. We were in our hotel 10 minutes after reaching the Gare Du Nord...and then we spread out all our stuff on the floor—maps, tube station maps and a list of places we wanted to visit. We started with the obvious: the Louvre. Then, we found our way to Angelina, the oldest tea house in Paris. We continued walking...to the Champs Élysées and looking up in the distance we saw the Eiffel Tower. Then it finally hit me: I was in Paris! We also visited Notre Dame, Moulin Rouge, and Montmartre. Paris is my city of impulse and indulgence and I want to come back with no agenda, and walk on the paths I didn't get a chance to, the first time around. Paris, I have a massive crush on you.

WHAT YOU NEED

BUTTER - 1/4 CUP
PEPPER - 4 PEPPERCORNS
THYME - 4 SPRIGS
BAY LEAF - 2
ONION - 4, SLICED IN RINGS
SALT - TO TASTE
DEMERARA SUGAR - 1 TBSP
FLOUR - 2 TBSP
RED WINE - 1 CUP
CHICKEN STOCK - 5 CUPS
GRUYÈRE CHEESE - 200 GM
BAGUETTE / KADAK PAO - 6-8 SLICES

HOW TO MAKE IT

- In a non-stick pan, add the butter and let it melt on low flame.
- Add the pepper, thyme and bay leaf.
- Set the flame on medium and add the onions. Add a pinch of salt and let the onions sweat.
- Add the Demerara sugar and cook the onions on medium flame for 30 minutes or till brown.
- Add the flour and cook for 10 minutes.
- Add the red wine and let the mixture simmer for 2 minutes.
- Add the stock and let the mixture simmer for 30 minutes.
- Preheat the oven to 190°C.
- Pour the prepared soup into an oven-proof soup bowl.
- Place a slice of the bread over the soup. Layer the bread with Gruyère cheese and bake the dish for 4-5 minutes till the cheese melts and the soup bubbles a bit.
- Serve hot.

ꜱʟ Kale Salad

I like this leaf; it's dark, tough, and it has a lot of possibilities. It may not be everybody's favourite munch, but it is mine. I so love the non-drama about it; it's like you either take me in or leave me out. It's my no-nonsense part of any salad, and frankly, it is not half as tough as it makes itself out to be. You see, a lot of things can be changed with the right amount of love.

WHAT YOU NEED

KALE - 70 GM
OLIVE OIL - 1 TBSP
WALNUTS - 10, CRUSHED
SUGAR - 25 GM
LIME JUICE - 1/2 TBSP
GRAPES - 10

HOW TO MAKE IT

- Take about 30 gm of kale leaves and smear a little olive oil with fingertips.
- Bake in a pre-heated oven at 175°C for 5 minutes.
- In a greased tray, arrange the crushed walnuts.
- In a small non-stick pan, on medium flame, heat the sugar till it melts and turns caramel in colour.
- Pour the caramelised sugar over the crushed walnuts.
- In another bowl, emulsify the lime juice and the olive oil.
- Roughly tear apart the non-cooked kale leaves.
- Gently massage the leaves with the lime and olive oil dressing.
- Mix with the baked kale leaves, toss in the grapes, and crush the caramelised walnuts.
- Serve.

IF YOU WANT TO TELL SOMEONE, HOW MUCH YOU LOVE THEM, BAKE THEM THIS.

ST Cheesy Potato Skins

This is something that everyone should make at least once a week, because then you will have to exercise a bit more!
But it's so much fun to make this dish, with kids or with friends, that it's completely addictive.
And I don't know anyone who does not like potatoes.

WHAT YOU NEED

OLIVE OIL - 4 TBSP
BUTTER - 2 TBSP
ONION - 3, CARAMELISED
SALT - A PINCH
SUGAR - 1 TSP
WATER - 2 TBSP
BALSAMIC VINEGAR - 1 TBSP
BIG POTATOES - 8
CHEDDAR CHEESE - 1 1/2 CUPS, GRATED
FRESH MOZZARELLA CHEESE - 1/2 CUP
SOUR CREAM - 1/2 CUP

HOW TO MAKE IT

- In a non-stick pan, add 1 tablespoon each of olive oil and butter.
- Add the onions and cook evenly till translucent. This might take 10-15 minutes. Sprinkle the onions with a little salt.
- Add the sugar, water, and balsamic vinegar to prevent the onions from getting burnt.
- Do not stir too often; the onions should turn brown.
- Cook for 20-30 minutes.
- Preheat the oven to 200°C.
- Wash and scrub the potatoes, smear with some olive oil and bake for 40 minutes.
- Take out the potatoes and allow them to cool down.
- Cut the potatoes in half and scoop out the flesh.
- Smear all sides of the potato skins with a mix of 1 tablespoon of olive oil and 1 tablespoon of butter.
- Bake for 8 minutes or till crisp.
- Take them out and fill generously with the grated Cheddar and mozzarella cheese.
- Bake for about 5 minutes at 200°C.
- Take them out and fill with a dollop of sour cream and caramelised onions.
- Serve hot.

Chicken Breast in Coconut Cream

MNV

Chicken breast is for the healthy; it's lean, but not mean. It's a very tricky part to cook; if you go overboard, you have full chances of making it taste like leather. So when you cook this, please do stick to the right amount of time. Timing is everything when you cook. This dish looks very fancy when presented, but is really easy, and the raw mango gives it a lovely tangy flavour. This is my version of something I learnt to cook at Tante Marie.

WHAT YOU NEED

CHICKEN BREAST - 4, BONELESS
RICOTTA CHEESE - 125 GM
CORIANDER - 3 TBSP, FINELY CHOPPED
MINT - 1 TBSP, FINELY CHOPPED
GREEN CHILLI - 1 MEDIUM, FINELY CHOPPED
RAW MANGO - 4 TBSP, FINELY CHOPPED
CUMIN - 1 TSP, DRY ROASTED AND POUNDED
OLIVE OIL - 2 TBSP
SALT - TO TASTE
BUTTER - 1 TSP
ONION - 4, FINELY SLICED
COCONUT CREAM - 250 ML
MILK CREAM - 200 ML
CINNAMON POWDER - 1/4 TSP

HOW TO MAKE IT

- Wash and slice the chicken breasts.
- Cover the sliced pieces with plastic and flatten the chicken by hitting it with a rolling pin.
- In a clean bowl, mix the ricotta cheese with the coriander, mint, chilli, raw mango and cumin.
- In the centre of each chicken breast, add a generous helping of the cheese mix.
- Fold the meat and secure with a string. Smear with some olive oil and salt.
- In a pan, add olive oil butter and sear the tied-up chicken breast for 2-3 minutes on either side.
- In a pre-heated oven, bake the chicken breasts for 15 minutes at 180°C.
- In a non-stick pan, sauté the onions till brown and crisp. Keep aside.
- In the same pan, add the coconut cream to the milk cream and add the cinnamon powder. Stir till the cream bubbles a bit.
- Pour the sauce over the cooked chicken.
- Garnish with onions and serve hot.

MY AUDREY HEPBURN VERSION OF THE SIMPLE CAULIFLOWER

MV Cauliflower Gratin

This is what I call my 'undercover food.' As a mum, I have learned various ways to make my kids eat vegetables. And this is one such 'undercover agent' that they completely love; it's wholesome and nutritious and totally yummy. With this dish that is devoured with great relish by my kids, I have bestowed myself with the title 'Mata Hari' of vegetables.

WHAT YOU NEED

CAULIFLOWER - 1 HEAD
BUTTER - 2 TBSP
FLOUR - 1 TBSP
MILK - 1 1/2 CUP
NUTMEG - 1/2 TSP
SALT - TO TASTE
PEPPER - TO TASTE
BRIE CHEESE - 1/4 CUP
GRUYÈRE CHEESE - 1/4 CUP
CHEDDAR CHEESE - 1/2 CUP
CREAM - 1/2 CUP
BREADCRUMBS - 3 TBSP
ALMOND FLAKES - A FEW

HOW TO MAKE IT

• Cook the cauliflower florets in boiling water for 15 minutes.
• Dunk in a bowl of ice water and keep aside.
• In a non-stick pan, on medium flame, add the butter and the flour.
• Cook for about 2-4 minutes.
• Add the milk, a little at a time, till you get a thick sauce.
• Add the nutmeg, salt and pepper.
• Add the different varieties of cheese and cream.
• Stir well till no lumps remain.
• Arrange the cauliflower florets in a baking tray.
• Pour the cheesy sauce over them.
• Sprinkle with the breadcrumbs and the almond flakes.
• Bake in a pre-heated oven at 175°C for 20 minutes or till brown.
• Serve hot.

Lemon Tart with Meringue

D

Sometimes, when life offers me lemons, what do I do? Simple. I make Lemon Meringue Tart! As you make it,
a definite aroma of lime wafts into your kitchen; it's fresh and simply seductive. I'm talking about sour-limes.
But everything that tastes sour in life does not necessarily have to be 'not tasty.' It all depends on what you do with it.
This Lemon Tart recipe is from the Tante Marie Recipe Book, and my principal Andrew was happy to share it with you.
So happy baking!

WHAT YOU NEED
(SHORT CRUST PASTRY)

FLOUR - 175 GM
SALT - A PINCH
BUTTER - 90 GM, CHILLED CUBES
CHILLED WATER - 5-7 TSP,

HOW TO MAKE IT

- Sift the flour and salt in a mixing bowl.
- Cut the butter into tiny cubes, and rub into flour, till it
  resembles breadcrumbs.
- Make a well in the centre and add the required water, and mix
  into a firm dough.
- Let it rest in the refrigerator for 20 minutes.
- You can divide this into 4 tartlets and bake it at 200°C for
  15-20 minutes.
- Or bake just one big tart for 20-30 minutes.

WHAT YOU NEED
(LEMON FILLING)

CORNFLOUR - 40 GM
WATER - 300 ML
BUTTER - 25 GM
LEMONS - 2
CASTER SUGAR - 200 GM
EGGS - 2, SEPARATED
EXTRA EGG WHITE - 1

HOW TO MAKE IT

- Blend cornflour with a little water and keep aside.
- Heat the remaining water.
- Pour the hot water onto the blended cornflour and mix well.
- Return the pan to the flame and simmer for 2-3 minutes.
- Remove pan from the heat, add butter, finely grated lemon zest,
  sugar and the eggs.
- Mix well and pour into the tart case.

HOW TO MAKE IT

- For the Meringue recipe, see page 88.
- Pour the lemon filling into the baked tarts.
- Pipe or smear the meringue over the filling.
- Cover completely.
- Bake in a pre-heated oven at 200°C for 20-30 minutes if it is one big tart or 8-12 minutes if they are small tartlets. Bake till the meringue turns slightly brown.
- Serve at room temperature.

October

SOUP PAK CHOI, TOFU, BURNT GARLIC,
EGG NOODLE CLEAR SOUP
SALAD MICRO GREEN SALAD
STARTER SOYA FLAVOURED EDAMAME BEANS
MAIN COURSE (NON-VEGETARIAN)
BHUTANESE LAMB
MAIN COURSE (VEGETARIAN)
VEGETABLE MOMOS
DESSERT
STICKY RICE WITH MANGO PUDDING

While I was growing up, South East Asian cuisine was a luxury—mostly confined to Chinese cuisine—and you could only eat it if you went to a fancy restaurant. The family would make an evening of it, dress up to the nines and go out for dinner. Later on, I realised that Chinese was not the only kind of Oriental cuisine available.

I love Thai food. It always puts me in holiday mode, diving into blue seas, smiling faces and beautiful eyes. Sawadeekhaap and the aroma of spicy prawn in red curry is something that can make me get out of my pajamas and book a ticket to Thailand at the drop of a hat. The sights and sounds there range from completely hectic to tranquil, just like their food. Then there is true blue Chinese food that is so sumptuous and finger-licking good that I'm completely confused about which type of Oriental food I like. My earliest memories still come from visiting China Town in Kolkata. My first introduction to the bylanes in the tanning community, and then the hunt for that elusive place on the first floor of a leather shop, where you get the most amazing wilted spinach with tofu. Oriental food in various other places around the world like in Korea, New York, San Francisco and Melbourne opened up a totally new set of taste buds.

I remember I was in Korea to interview Enrique Iglesias, and we went out for food with the crew. The table where we sat had a Lazy-Suzy turntable in the middle and by the time I would make up my mind and reach out to a dish, the table would turn. I starved and ate fast food for dinner.

When I visited Bhutan in May 2012 for the literature festival, because Arshad was invited to speak there, I had a splendid time. I went there purely by chance, changing my mind in favour of travelling at the very last minute. I believe Bhutan was a place I needed to go to so I could 'walk with my dragons.' Like anyone else, I had my own personal monsters to deal with and over there I walked with them, on the mountainside besides brooks and majestic stupas and in fields of wild flowers. I realised that the dragons who walked with me were not half as worrisome as

I thought them to be. They were sweet, loving and had beautiful eyes and naughty grins. But I bid them farewell, hugged them tight, kissed them deeply and let them go. The land of the Buddha brought back my crazy laughter. I also met the most wonderful set of crazy people from back home in the midst of this beautiful valley—Wendell Rodricks, Mushtaq Sheikh, Shakun Batra, Ajay Mago, Preeti Bhutani and Tisca Chopra (who I had known for a large part of my life). We gravitated towards one another and then like a motley crew we walked around having the time of our lives. I don't remember not having a smile on my face or cracking up at the drop of a hat. Maybe there was something in the air or maybe it was just a fusion of all our energies, that crazily combusted into laughing gas.

I learnt how to make Bhutanese food from a local chef there; Ema Datshi—a dish made with local cheese, corn rice, that you just cannot stop eating and the Bhutanese lamb. We were all filled with a sense of *joie de vivre* that made us glow like fireflies...Ajay Mago, Shakun Batra, Arshad and I walked up 900 metres to Taktsang or 'Tiger's Nest' to visit one of the oldest meditation caves in Bhutan overlooking the Paro valley. This climb is a test, not of strength, but your mind and will power. It's really tough because the incline is very steep but we just had to do it. After the first half an hour, we were all wondering what on earth we had got ourselves into. Shakun said, 'There is no hell in Bhutan. If you are bad, you come back as a donkey that carries people up this mountain.' And I think because of the lack of oxygen and the tough climb, we were all delirious and began laughing hysterically in the middle of bouts of breathlessness. As for the climb, it was completely worth the effort. There is nothing that prepares you for the site of this monastery perched on the side of the granite face of this majestic mountain and the sense of calm and peace that accost you ever so tenderly.

This menu is a mix of different flavours of the Orient. It's rustic, beautifully balanced and you might call it my walk through the ingredients I love.

Pak Choi, Tofu, Burnt Garlic, Egg Noodle Clear Soup

The main ingredient here is the galangal with the delicate balance of the lemongrass. It smells and tastes fantastic and the buttery tasting silken tofu just seals the deal.

WHAT YOU NEED

PAK CHOI - 1 BIG BULB
OLIVE OIL - 2 TBSP
GARLIC - 10 BIG CLOVES
CHICKEN STOCK
    OR VEGETABLE STOCK - 5 CUPS
EGG NOODLES - 125 GM
LEMONGRASS - 1 STALK
LIME LEAVES - 2
GALANGAL - 1 THUMB-SIZE PIECE
SILKEN TOFU - 150 GM, CUT INTO
    BIG CUBES
YELLOW PEPPER - 1/2, DICED INTO
    TINY PIECES
RED PEPPER - 1/2, DICED INTO
    TINY PIECES
SESAME OIL - 1 TBSP

HOW TO MAKE IT

- Sear the Pak Choi in olive oil. Do not let it wilt completely.
- Keep aside and add the garlic in the same oil.
- Cook till toasty brown.
- Pour 3 cups of stock into a pot and boil.
- Add the egg noodles, lemongrass, lime leaves and galangal and let the mixture simmer till the noodles are soft and cooked. This will take about 8-10 minutes.
- Strain the soup contents and reserve the flavoured stock.
- Keep the noodles aside, discarding the lemongrass, galangal and lime leaves.
- In a clean bowl, add the remaining stock. Bring to a boil.
- Add Pak Choi and tofu and the peppers and lower the flame. Let the liquid simmer for 3 minutes.
- Add sesame oil and let the mixture simmer for half a minute more.
- Add the noodles back into the pot.
- Serve hot.

SL Micro Green Salad

More often, than less, we complicate most of our life. If things are simple, we end up wondering
what's wrong and why it is not complicated. But, trust me with this salad. It can't get any more to the point.
It's the easiest of ingredients that emulsify into the nicest flavourful dressing you could taste,
and the crisp micro greens know exactly how to twirl in happily.

WHAT YOU NEED

MICRO GREENS - 150 GM
CHERRY TOMATO- 6, HALVED
GINGER JUICE - 1 TSP
SESAME OIL - 1 TSP
SOYA - 1 TSP

HOW TO MAKE IT

• Wash all the micro greens.
• Pour the dressing after mixing all the ingredients.
• Serve immediately.

I HAVE NOT YET MET A FRESH GREEN SALAD THAT I DONT LIKE

ST Soya Flavoured Edamame Beans

These beans always remind me of Jalan Alor and the time I spent with Mini and Yudi in the rainforest of Taman Negara. It's one of the most impulsive and fun holidays I have had. Snakes fell out from the trees and geckos accompanied us as if they were our pets. We trekked to the hanging bridge alone in the middle of the rainforest, and had a grand feast of amazing Malaysian food on a weekend.

WHAT YOU NEED

DEMERARA SUGAR - 2 TBSP
SOYA SAUCE - 2 TBSP
WATER - 2 TBSP
VEGETABLE OIL - 1 TBSP
SESAME OIL - 1 TBSP
GINGER-GARLIC PASTE - 1/2 TSP
CHILLI FLAKES - 1 TSP
EDAMAME BEANS - 2 CUPS,
    PARBOILED & DRAINED

HOW TO MAKE IT

- Mix the Demerara sugar, soya sauce and water. Keep aside.
- In a non-stick pan, on medium flame, add the oils, ginger-garlic paste and chilli flakes.
- Sauté by stirring continuously.
- Add the beans and stir well.
- Add the sugar-soya-water mixture and increase the heat.
- Toss the beans and mix. Let this mix reduce till a glaze forms over the beans.
- Serve hot.

∿ Bhutanese Lamb

I remember the first time I bit into this succulent lamb with corn rice...I was silenced. This was so full of flavour that I just had to learn how to prepare this dish. And frankly, once I decide to do something, I can be quite unstoppable. What I learnt from a chef in Bhutan was that the best way to keep the flavour is to keep it simple. Back to basics, actually! So this lamb is very basic and this recipe has no tricks or any secret cooking techniques. This dish is actually very much like the people of Bhutan, simple and full of flavour. It's so basic, yet, is one of my favourite lamb preparations, and the rice noodles just add the right amount of carbs and satisfaction.

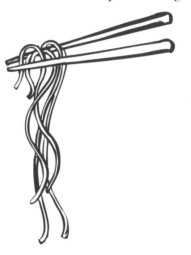

WHAT YOU NEED

WATER - 3 CUPS
VEGETABLE OIL - 3 TBSP + 1 TBSP
LAMB - 500 GM, CUBED
SALT - TO TASTE
ONION - 2, SLICED
GREEN CHILLI - 1
RED CHILLI POWDER - 1 TSP
TOMATO - 3, DICED
RICE NOODLE - 1 PACKET

HOW TO MAKE IT

- Take a pressure cooker, add water along with 1 tablespoon oil.
- Add the lamb and a pinch of salt.
- Cook on low flame for 20 minutes and wait for 1 whistle.
  (If you are not using a pressure cooker, cook for about
  40 minutes with 4 cups of water on medium flame after the first
  big boil.)
- Put the remaining oil in a thick-bottomed pan.
- Add the onions, fresh green chilli, red chilli powder and cook
  till the onions are translucent.
- Add the tomatoes and cook for about 15-20 minutes or till the
  oil separates.
- Add the mutton and stir well. Bring to a boil.
- Soak rice noodles in water.
- Drain and add to the mutton broth.
- Serve immediately with a dollop of butter.

EVERY TIME I HAVE
A MORSEL OF THIS,
I WANT TO TREK BACK
WITH AJAY, SHAKUN
AND ARSHAD
TO TIGER'S-NEST

MV Vegetable Momos

I think the day I learnt to make momos from my friend Banita (who makes the best momos this side of the globe), my little Zeke's and Zene's dreams came true. Children are so sweet. It takes such basic stuff to make them happy.
Making momos has always frightened me, but with practice it gets slightly easy.
Thanks Bani for sharing this recipe with me.

WHAT YOU NEED
(FILLING)

CABBAGE - 1 CUP, FINELY CHOPPED
ONION - 3/4 CUP, FINELY CHOPPED
CARROT - 3/4 CUP, FINELY CHOPPED
CORIANDER - 1/4 CUP, FINELY CHOPPED
GARLIC - 1/2 TSP, GRATED
GINGER - 1 TSP, GRATED
SALT - TO TASTE
SESAME OIL - 2 TBSP
VEGETABLE OIL - 1/3 CUP
DIM SUM SHEETS - 12-18

HOW TO MAKE IT

- Add the salt to the cabbage and keep aside. After 20 minutes, drain all the water from the cabbage by squeezing it tight.
- Add the remaining vegetables.
- Add salt to taste.
- Add the oils and mix well.
- Take spoonfuls of the mixture and place onto the dim sum sheets. Make little parcels and seal with water.
- Steam for 12-15 minutes (for momos that are about 2-inches in size).

WHAT YOU NEED
(CHILLI SAUCE)

KASHMIRI CHILLI - 4, 3-DESEEDED
TOMATO - 4, PEELED
GARLIC - 2 FULL, GRATED
SALT - TO TASTE

HOW TO MAKE IT

- Soak the Kashmiri chillies in warm water.
- Drain the water before using.
- In a mixer, grind the tomatoes, garlic and the Kashmiri chillies.
- Add salt to taste.
- Serve with hot steaming dim sums.

Sticky Rice with Mango Pudding

Sticky rice and mango always transport me straight to Thailand. The bustling streets, the din, the food vendors, the fake bags being sold on the sidewalk, throngs of people eating, talking, walking...it's a city that is always on the go. And then while you are in the middle of this frenzy, you suddenly meet this smiling wrinkled face beckoning you to a bowl full of warm sticky rice with yummy golden mangoes sitting on it. A bite into this is heaven in a bowl.

WHAT YOU NEED

STICKY RICE - 1 CUP, UNCOOKED
WATER - 1 1/2 CUPS
COCONUT MILK - 3 1/2 CUPS
DEMERARA SUGAR - 4 TBSP
CONDENSED MILK - 50 ML
ALPHONSO MANGOES - 2-3
SESAME SEEDS - 2 TBSP

HOW TO MAKE IT

• Soak the washed rice in water for 2-4 hours.
• Add 1½ cups of coconut milk and the demerara sugar.
• Cook on medium flame for about 15-20 minutes or till cooked.
• Cover and leave aside to cool down.
• In a non-stick pan, add the remaining coconut milk and the condensed milk.
• Cook on a low flame. Let the mixture thicken.
• Scoop the cooled rice on a plate.
• Place the mangoes and top with the coconut milk sauce, which can be served warm or cold.
• Sprinkle with toasted sesame seeds for garnish.
• Serve.

November

SOUP CREAMY PRAWN SPAGHETTI SOUP
SALAD BAKED SWEET POTATO WITH
ARUGULA LEAVES
STARTER CHEESY CHOUX PASTRY
MAIN COURSE (NON-VEGETARIAN)
SALT-BAKED FISH
MAIN COURSE (VEGETARIAN) BAKED VEGETABLES
DESSERT CHOCO-OOZING MUFFINS

It's her birthday on November 26. Yes, she is lucky that she is a Sagittarian like me, two years younger, braver and more talented than I could ever be. She is my younger sister Juliet.

We were sitting one day discussing why we don't have pet names and I was reading an *Archie* comic, so I called her Juggie and she did not have a name for me. She kept saying 'I don't like it' and 'don't call me that', but the 'witchy' elder sister that I am, I kept teasing her and today my lovely and darling younger sister is known as 'Juggie' by me and all my friends. We have fought, pulled each other's hair and screamed and not talked and had a volatile time, but if I had to choose again, I would want her to be my sister again.

She was always the brave one; nothing, and no one, frightened her and I really looked up to her. She has loved me and has been there for me always. She now lives in Dallas and has started life all over again and makes the word 'multi-task' sound like putty, compared to what all she juggles.

Daughter, sister, mum, friend, driver, cook, teacher, cleaner, barber, laundry-person, iron-person, party-planner, and entertainer and so on... Oh! She is also a full-fledged photographer.

How she does everything single-handedly is a complete wonder. But every time we go over to meet her and the family, we have the most wonderful time. She has had more faith in me than I had in myself and the reason I was ever in MTV is because she pushed me to go and looked after my puppies Betty-Boo and Ninja despite being petrified of dogs. She thought that I would be brilliant, even though I was clueless.

You know you can choose your friends, but family, you have no choice there, and I just feel blessed to have Juliet as my sister. She has always been a rock, a bridge and an armour all rolled into one. And nothing would get her more enraged than if you messed with her family.

She loved her pet rabbits as much as she was petrified of dogs. She is still learning to swim but nothing stops her from putting skates on and going crazy with her kids. She would drive mum mad with the distances she went; she had a bike and used to take me as well, with me behind her.

Those were fun days that have stayed with me; there have been sad times too, but we just stuck together and walked ahead. That's what you do in life. That's what family does, you stick together, through thick and thin, whether you agree with one another or not. You run with your flock.

My sister is like a little tigress, you mess with her family and you will have to leave the jungle. Juggie, I love you.

SP Creamy Prawn Spaghetti Soup

This is super indulgent in terms of taste and is very satisfying; it's the kind of soup that looks at you saying,
'I know you want me'. This is just the kind of soup my sister would devour, without blinking an eye.
So, here's to indulgence.

WHAT YOU NEED

SPAGHETTI - 75 GM

OIL - 2 TBSP

BUTTER - 2 TBSP

GARLIC - 2 CLOVES

ONION - 1, CUBED

PEPPER - TO TASTE

PRAWNS - 12 JUMBO PRAWNS

ALL-PURPOSE FLOUR - 1 TBSP

POTATO - 1, CUBED

CHICKEN STOCK - 4 CUPS

CREAM - 75 ML

SALT - TO TASTE

HOW TO MAKE IT

- Cook the spaghetti as per package instructions and keep aside.
- In a non-stick pan add the oil and the butter.
- Let the mix sizzle and add the garlic.
- Sauté for 30 seconds, add the onion and cook for a minute.
- Grind fresh pepper and add.
- Add the deveined cleaned prawns and cook on high flame for 45 seconds on either side. Do not cook fully; take out the prawns and keep aside.
- Add the flour and cook well for about 2 minutes.
- Add the potato and cook for 5 minutes.
- When the mix turns brown, add 1 cup of stock. Cover and cook for 10-15 minutes.
- When the potato is fully cooked, add the remaining stock and bring to a boil.
- Add the prawns and the cream. Stir the broth well.
- Add the spaghetti and mix well.
- Stir well with a spaghetti spoon.
- Ladle out in bowls and serve piping hot.

SL Baked Sweet Potato with Arugula Leaves

I'm addicted to arugula leaves; the slightly bitter taste is something that completely appeals to my taste buds. When mixed with sweet potato, it is such a basic combination that it can't go wrong. The baked potato crisps are lightly chilli-flavoured, yet sweet and are just lovely with the arugula leaves.
If I had my way, I would eat these leaves with everything. Have you ever tried mixing these raw leaves in hot rice, a bowl of hot pasta or just deep frying them as garnish? Try it out, thank me later.

WHAT YOU NEED
(SALAD)

SWEET POTATO - 200 GM
OLIVE OIL - 1 TBSP
PAPRIKA - A PINCH
ARUGULA LEAVES - 70 GM
SALT - TO TASTE

WHAT YOU NEED
(DRESSING)

DIJON MUSTARD - 1 TSP
MAPLE SYRUP - 1 TSP
WHITE WINE VINEGAR - 1 TSP

HOW TO MAKE IT

• Wash, peel and finely slice the sweet potato.
• Smear with olive oil and sprinkle paprika.
• Bake in a pre-heated oven at 175°C for 16-17 minutes, but be careful not to burn them.
• Mix the dressing ingredients and pour over the Arugula leaves.
• Place the crispy baked sweet potato over the prepared dressing and serve.

MY TYPE OF LEAF

LITTLE MONSTERS OF YUM

ST Cheesy Choux Pastry

This is just a hit. It cannot go wrong; the crispy feel of the pastry and the indulgent cheesiness are perfect for a nibble. You can stuff it with cream cheese or chutney or just let it be. It's lovely, served directly from an oven onto the table, and no, I won't take offence even if you eat it with ketchup. Just don't do that in front of me!

HOW TO MAKE IT

- In a non-stick medium-size saucepan, add the water, butter, and salt.
- Bring to a boil on high flame.
- Turn off the heat and add the flour all at once. Stir rapidly.
- Put the mix back on medium flame. Keep stirring, till the mix forms a dough ball.
- Continue to cook for 5 minutes.
- Remove the pan from the heat and keep aside to cool down.
- Keep stirring the dough till cooled, before you add the eggs one at a time.
- Stir continuously after each addition, until the eggs get incorporated in the dough. The dough should become a bit sticky and creamy.
- Stir in the grated cheese and the pepper.
- Preheat the oven to 200°C.
- Spoon out small balls of the dough onto a lined baking sheet, not too close to one another (they will increase in volume once puffed up).
- Cook in the oven for 10 minutes at 200°C.
- Lower the heat to 175°C and cook for another 15-20 minutes or until puffed up and slightly golden brown.
- Let it cool. Serve it stuffed with some cream cheese and fresh vegetables.

WHAT YOU NEED

WATER - 1 CUP
BUTTER - 115 GM
SALT - TO TASTE
ALL-PURPOSE FLOUR - 1 CUP
EGG - 5
CHEDDAR CHEESE - 100 GM, GRATED
PEPPER - TO TASTE, FRESHLY GROUND

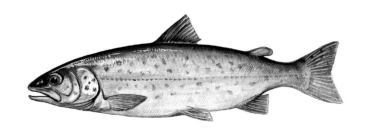

MNV Salt-Baked Fish

This was one of the many last recipes I shot for my book and was the easiest. Fresh fish and lots of salt are what you will require. It's such a pleasure to cook this because it is simple and yet there is so much drama around it, that makes it the person baking it look like a Michelin star chef. Timing is supreme in this recipe, and that's what converts this simple preparation into a star attraction. It's ideal for a summer afternoon.

WHAT YOU NEED
(COOKING CRUST)

ROCK SALT - 3 KG
EGG WHITES - 4, LIGHTLY BEATEN
LEMON JUICE - 6, JUICE SQUEEZED

HOW TO MAKE IT

- Prepare the salt crust by adding the egg whites and the lemon juice to the salt.
- Pour in a little water (if needed).
- Scrunch together till it reminds you of wet sand. (But one that smells tasty.)

WHAT YOU NEED
(SALT-BAKED FISH)

RAVA FISH - 3 PIECES, 300-350 GM EACH,
    GUTTED AND WASHED AND NOT SCALED
FLAT LEAF PARSLEY - 50 GM
OLIVE OIL - 50 ML
BAY LEAF - 3
BUTTER - 3 TBSP

HOW TO MAKE IT

- Preheat the oven to 220°C.
- Do not scale the fish. Clean the insides by making a small incision next to the stomach.
- Stuff the cleaned cavity of the fish with parsley, a few drops of oil and a thin wedge of lime.
- Smear the fish with the olive oil and keep aside.
- Put a layer of salt on the bottom of the baking dish.
- Place the fish on this mattress of salt and cover the fish with the rest of the prepared salt. Pat gently, add bay leaves, the squeezed out lemon skins and fresh herb stalks.
- Bake for 20 minutes in a pre-heated oven at 220°C.
- Take out the tray and crack open the hardened shell. The skin peels off with the salt. If that does not happen, take the skin off and eat the fish with melted butter poured on it, with a squeeze of lime.

THIS DISH WILL MAKE EVERYONE BELIEVE
THAT YOU HAVE SLOGGED IT OUT IN THE
KITCHEN WHILE YOU WERE ACTUALLY
DRINKING A GLASS OF BUBBLY

MV Baked Vegetables

This is my all-time favourite way to eat vegetables because each vegetable, even after you cook it,
does not taste like the spice you add into it, but instead, tasted like its natural self. And that is the best part.
So if you are up to some 'take me as I am' kind of dish, look no further.

WHAT YOU NEED

AUBERGINE - 1, MEDIUM-SIZE

POTATO - 2, HALVED

PEPPER - 2, DESEEDED AND CUT IN BIG CHUNKS

SQUASH - 100 GM, CUT IN BIG CHUNKS

COURGETTE - 1, THICKLY SLICED

CARROT - 1, CLEANED AND SLICED OR CUT IN CHUNKS

TOMATO - 4, HALVED

OLIVE OIL - ENOUGH TO MOISTEN THE VEGETABLES

OREGANO - 3 TBSP

ROSEMARY - 3 TBSP

ROCK SALT - TO TASTE

BLUE CHEESE- AS GARNISH

HOW TO MAKE IT

• Cut all the vegetables in like-sized chunks.
• Pour the olive oil.
• Sprinkle the oregano, rosemary and rock salt over
  the vegetables.
• Bake in a pre-heated oven at 190°C for 25 minutes.
• Serve hot with a sprinkle of blue cheese.

Choco-Oozing Muffins

D

There is really nothing simpler than chocolate. You give chocolate to the people you love and yet, you realise that it's just a box of chocolates. Chocolate is 'complicated', and maybe, that's why I love it. Just follow this recipe blindly, it never goes wrong. The nice thing would be if you can bake this fresh. It's always nice to have your kitchen enveloped with the aroma of a chocolate cake in baking. The chocolate oozing out, when you scoop into the muffin, is pure bliss.

WHAT YOU NEED

COOKING CHOCOLATE - 200 GM, CHOPPED
BUTTER - 200 GM
EGG - 3
GRANULATED SUGAR - 1/2 CUP
FLOUR - 1/3 CUP
CREAM CHEESE - 2 TBSP, HEAPED

HOW TO MAKE IT

- Preheat the oven to 250°C for 30 minutes before you start baking.
- Melt the cooking chocolate in a small vessel over a pan of boiling water and keep aside to cool down. Once cooled, add the butter and stir well till blended.
- In another bowl, beat the eggs and the granulated sugar till the mix turns white.
- Add the chocolate-butter mix and add the flour.
- Add the cream cheese.
- Divide the mix into 7 small foil containers and bake in an oven for 8 minutes at 250°C.
- Serve immediately.

December

DRINK MULLED WINE
SALAD WINTER SALAD
STARTER CHICKEN HONEY
MUSTARD SAUSAGES
MAIN COURSE (NON-VEGETARIAN)
BAKED CHICKEN
MAIN COURSE (VEGETARIAN)
PANCAKES WITH AUBERGINE
AND PEPPERONATA SAUCE
DESSERT TIRAMISU

Now that it's nearly the end of the book, let me be very honest... I never thought I would ever write a book. This whole experience has been kind of crazy. And in a way, I relived my entire life by the time I actually reached December in my book. I remembered a lot of paths in life, that I walked on and reconnected with a lot of people I walked with.

Every year, when December is nearing, a million thoughts run through my head: Gosh this year has sped away and what have I done this year? How many friends are still my friends? Have I been a good person this year? Can I give the kids all the toys I want to give them for Christmas or is Santa supposed to be a 'little-not-so-happy,' so he got them a lot but not everything on the list?

When I get into the Christmas groove, even I'm busy sending letters to Santa that are delivered to him through telepathy, asking for various things I would like in my life. The secret is to 'never ask for anything materialistic'.

And then I sit down with my Christmas menu that I decide on, and scrap, many times over. Why, because that's how I am, I'm always changing my mind. Mercurial, that's what I am sometimes! But the one thing that does not change is the feeling of Christmas that surrounds me like a warm comfortable familiar blanket.

I love this time of the year; it reminds me of my family. My grandma, and her sister, Aunty Carola, who was a nun, would make the most amazing puff pastry; they would toil on from morning, discussing their younger days. My mum would make Christmas sweets that were distributed on Christmas morning. We hoped that my dad would be able to come back from work for Christmas. Uncle Casho would land on Christmas morning with loads of goodies. There was midnight mass to attend, my sister and I trying to curl our hair (it was the only time we were allowed to use hair spray and this curler set my dad had bought), singing in the choir, and running back home, because mum would say, 'I think Santa is home'.

How can Christmas not be special; it's the time of the year that makes all wrong, right. It heals hearts with love. This month I cook with abandon. And I love my home bustling with my family and friends. The tree has gifts under it. My home is filled with laughter and mirth; it's the only way one should end a year.

This menu comes straight from my heart, from my kitchen to yours. Merry Christmas and a Happy New Year.

DR Mulled Wine

I know, my bay never really does have the right kind of temperature for warm mulled wine.
But I think in December, it just feels so right. I love this recipe. It's yummy and so apt for Christmas that
you just have to include it in your Christmas menu. It smells of good tidings, of love, peace and all that Christmas stands for.
It also reminds me of London and Christmas carols on the streets. I know it is easier to just serve red wine when you have a
crowd of people in your home and you are cooking and being a hostess. But with this, it's just a little extra special.

WHAT YOU NEED

ORANGE - 2, PEELED & THEN JUICED
DEMERARA SUGAR - 1/2 CUP
WATER - 1 CUP
VANILLA BEAN - 1
CLOVES - 4
STAR ANISE - 3
CINNAMON STICK - 1
ALLSPICE - 2 TSP, GROUND
NUTMEG - 2 TSP, GRATED
FULL-BODIED RED WINE - 1 BOTTLE
COGNAC - 1/2 CUP
LEMON - 1, PEELED

HOW TO MAKE IT

- Peel the orange skin.
- In a non-stick pot, on medium flame, mix the sugar and water.
- Add the zest and juice of the 2 oranges.
- Add the vanilla bean, cloves, star anise, cinnamon stick, allspice and nutmeg gratings.
- Bring to a boil.
- After about 25 minutes, add about half a cup of wine.
- Simmer for 20 minutes more to get a syrupy consistency, infused with all the flavours.
- Add the remaining wine and the cognac and gently bring to a simmer for about 2 minutes.
- Do not overheat as the alcohol content will dissipate.
- Ladle into glasses and serve warm.
- You can also add seasonal fruits to the warm mulled wine. Let the preparation sit for 15 minutes.
- Always serve warm, but do not reheat.

SL Winter Salad

My Christmas menu is never complete without this salad; it's a must-have and goes beautifully with the wine. It's full of fruits, nuts and complements the whole ambience of Christmas. Don't feel shy to throw in a bunch of more strawberries, tis' the season to be merry.

WHAT YOU NEED

OLIVE OIL – 3 TBSP
BALSAMIC VINEGAR – 1 AND 1/2 TBSP
ORANGE – 1
STRAWBERRIES – 6
ARUGULA LEAVES – 100 GM
POMEGRANATE – 1/2
FETA CHEESE – 50 GM
PINE NUTS – 3 TBSP
MIXED SEEDS – 2 TBSP

HOW TO MAKE IT

- Emulsify the olive oil and balsamic vinegar and keep aside.
- Segment the orange and keep aside.
- Hull and cut the strawberries into medium pieces.
- Add the emulsified balsamic-oil mix to the arugula leaves and toss them with your hands.
- Add the oranges, strawberries, pomegranate kernels, crumbled feta cheese and the mixed seeds.
- Garnish with feta cheese and toasted pine nuts.
- The salad is ready to eat.

ST Chicken Honey Mustard Sausages

This is something I had at a restaurant once. I came home and tried out various permutations and combinations, and this one works all the time. The kids love it, the adults love it, and I make this fresh, just before I serve it. This is easy as you are just putting things together; but what comes out after it is cooked, is not something you will find on a shelf at a gourmet store.

WHAT YOU NEED

CHICKEN SAUSAGES - 200 GM
FRESHLY GROUND MUSTARD POWDER - 2 TBSP
VEGETABLE OIL - 1 1/2 TBSP
BUTTER - 1 TBSP, HEAPED
HONEY - 2 TBSP
SOYA SAUCE - 1 TBSP
CHILLI FLAKES- A PINCH

HOW TO MAKE IT

• Cut the sausages in 1-inch thick pieces.
• Smear mustard on the sausages.
• Heat a heavy-bottomed non-stick pan.
• Add the oil and butter.
• Add the sausages, honey, chilli flakes and soya sauce.
• Cook for about 12 minutes on medium flame, till the sausages are sticky and have a dark glaze.
• Serve hot.

ⓜⓝⓥ Baked Chicken

As a kid, no occassion was complete without a baked bird on the table. It's my 'go to' food, for all things connected to family, friends and celebration. My mum is a pro at this. This is one of the first dishes I learnt to make and it came out fantastic. When in doubt, this is what I bake. It's really easy but looks like a formidable task. I'm liberal with the butter, because the meat gets really succulent and flavoured, and the aroma of melted butter is very inviting.

WHAT YOU NEED

WHOLE CHICKEN - 1 1/2 KG
OIL - 1 TBSP
RAISINS - 10
CASHEW - 10
ONION - 1 SMALL, FINELY CHOPPED
GREEN CHILLI - 1
GARLIC - 5 CLOVES
SAUSAGE MEAT (MUTTON/CHICKEN) - 25 GM
CHICKEN LIVER - THAT COMES ALONG WITH
    THE CHICKEN, CHOPPED
BREADCRUMBS - 2 TBSP
FLAT-LEAF PARSLEY - 2 TBSP, FINELY
    CHOPPED
BUTTER - 25 GM
EAST-INDIAN BOTTLE MASALA - 1 TSP
CHICKEN BACON - 12 STRIPS

HOW TO MAKE IT

- Wash the whole chicken and keep aside. Allow the water to completely drain.
- In a non-stick pan, add ½ tablespoon of oil. Add the raisins. Once the raisins are cooked and puffed out, take them out and keep aside.
- Add the cashews and fry till golden brown. Take them out and keep aside.
- Sauté the onion, add chilli and garlic. Cook for a minute.
- Add the sausage meat and once cooked, add the chicken liver.
- Cook for about a minute or till the liver is visibly cooked. Keep aside to cool down.
- When cooled, add the breadcrumbs, parsley, raisins and cashews to the liver mix.
- Mix the butter and the East-Indian Bottle Masala. Smear the chicken inside out with the prepared mix.
- Put the stuffing under the skin of the chicken belly, gently. (If this seems tough, put the stuffing in the stomach cavity.)
- Place the chicken bacon strips over the whole chicken and cover the chest, stomach and the legs completely.
- Bake the chicken for 1 hour and 20 minutes in a pre-heated oven at 190°C or till the chicken is dark brown.
- Serve hot.

MV Pancakes With Aubergine And Pepperonata Sauce

Every year when I'm trying to get a super menu in place, the last thing on my mind is vegetarian. That was never very big in my growing up years. Vegetarian was mostly an aside to the meat main course. There is something very royal about this chubby pulpy purple vegetable. The only reason I make vegetarian food for Christmas is my friend, Jaya. And I have to keep upping the flavour and taste since she is used to really awesome vegetarian food.

WHAT YOU NEED
(PANCAKES)

FLOUR - 100 GM
BAKING POWDER - 1/4 TSP
CARBONATE OF SODA - 1/4 TSP
CAYENNE PEPPER - 1/4 TSP
SALT - TO TASTE
BUTTERMILK - 1 CUP
MILK - 1/2 CUP
EGG - 1
BUTTER - 1 TBSP MELTED + FOR FRYING

WHAT YOU NEED
(AUBERGINE ROLLS)

AUBERGINE - 500 GM
OLIVE OIL - 50 ML
FETA CHEESE - 250 GM
FRESH MOZZARELLA
CHEESE - 6-8

WHAT YOU NEED
(PEPPERONATA SAUCE)

OLIVE OIL - 2 TBSP
GARLIC - 6 CLOVES
GREEN CHILLI - 1
ONION - 1, BIG SIZED
CHILLI FLAKES - 1 TSP
TOMATO - 4, MEDIUM-SIZED
RED PEPPER - 1
YELLOW PEPPER - 1
WATER - 100 ML
WHITE WINE - 100 ML
BASIL - A HANDFUL, HAND TORN

HOW TO MAKE IT

- Mix all the dry ingredients and keep aside.
- Mix all the wet ingredients except the butter reserved for frying.
- Add the wet ingredients to the dry ingredients.
- In a non-stick pan, smear butter.
- Add a ladle of the batter and cook on medium flame for about 2 minutes on either side or till golden brown.
- Keep aside to cool down.

HOW TO MAKE IT

- Preheat the oven and set it on the grill mode to 190° C.
- Slice the aubergines into pieces that are ¼-inch thick.
- Smear oil and grill on either side for about 5 minutes.
- Keep aside to cool down.

HOW TO MAKE IT

- In a non-stick thick-bottomed pan, add the oil. Add the garlic and chilli and sauté for about 30 seconds.
- Add the onion and cook till soft and translucent.
- Add the chilli flakes and stir well.
- Add the tomatoes, peppers and water.
- Bring to a simmer on medium flame for about 10 minutes.
- Add the white wine and let the sauce simmer (covered) for 10 minutes.
- Add the basil, stir in and keep aside.
- Adjust the seasoning.

ASSEMBLE

- Place the pancake in a small baking mould.
- Roll the crumbled feta cheeese into the aubergines.
- Place about 3 pieces on the pancake.
- Spoon a ladle of the pepperonata sauce on the aubergine and add a slice of fresh mozzarella cheese.
- Bake in the oven for 15-20 minutes or till the mozzarella has melted and the pepperonata sauce is bubbling without drying up.

Tiramisu

This literally means pick me up. I think it's the cutest bit of information I came across in a very long time, and I wanted to share this with you. This dish was actually first made in a brothel in the north of Italy. The kick of the alcohol and the coffee was supposed to be a great combination for a totally amorous evening. So, it's actually a dish that is naughty, sinful, and was meant for the ones who were up to no good. It is a lovely dessert that requires the right amount of whipping, whisking and alcohol. I decided to tweak it with a bit of Amarula because I am in love with its flavour. I guess you can say, it is just what you need to complete a well-cooked Christmas meal with a little bit of recklessness.

WHAT YOU NEED

ESPRESSO COFFEE - 260 ML +
    2 TBSP SUGAR
RED RUM - 2 TBSP
EGGS - 2, SEPARATED
CASTOR SUGAR - 4 TBSP,
MASCARPONE CHEESE - 250 GM
AMARULA - 3 TBSP
WHIPPED CREAM - 1/2 CUP
SAVIORDI BISCUITS - 18 PIECES

HOW TO MAKE IT

- Make 260 ml of espresso and add 2 tablespoons of sugar.
- Add the rum and refrigerate. Allow the concoction to chill.
- Whisk the egg yolks and 2 tablespoons of sugar till the batter turns light in colour, becomes creamy and thick.
- Add the Mascarpone cheese to the yolk and sugar mixture.
- Whisk the Amarula.
- Beat the egg whites to stiff peaks and add the remaining sugar, ½ teaspoon of sugar at a time, and let the batter achieve a meringue-like consistency. (This is something I did because it helps to keep the mixture slightly thick.)
- Whip the cream.
- Fold the cream into the Mascarpone-yolk mixture.
- Fold the egg whites into the mix, carefully.
- Dip one biscuit at a time into the coffee-rum mix, carefully, for not more than 3 seconds.
- Break them into two and place at the base of the glass.
- Spoon a dollop or more of the Mascarpone mix onto the glass.
- Do this with 2 more layers of biscuits and end with the cream.
- Chill this mix for at least 6-8 hours before you serve.

IF YOU ARE GOING TO SIN
THEN YOU BETTER MAKE
IT WORTH YOUR WHILE.

Grandma Agnes and Grandma Rosemary. I know they must be really happy that I have finally started to cook. And I'm sure they are steering me in the right direction, every time I try something new.

My mum, who I harass no end to give me her recipes of the dishes that I ate as a kid. She has the patience of a Pope, so she indulges me, and frankly, I still do not make prawn curry like she does. She wanted me to learn cooking and finally I have. She has never cooked in measurements of spoons and teaspoons, but there's magic in her touch.

My dad, for cooking for us when we were kids. He introduced us to new stuff, brought us the best cheese and cured meats, got me my masalas and always bought the best fish at the most amazing prices. From him I learned that you can bargain in the fish market without saying a word and yet come home with a loot. He is the one who introduced me to bread-making and he kneads dough like no other.

Juliet, for always standing by me, no matter what; for always thinking that I deserve better and believing it; for always being the only person in the world who loves me more than I could ever love. You are the bravest girl I know. Thank you for being my sister in this lifetime; I must have done something amazing in my past life to have you.

All the boys in my life, for always behaving like they have never eaten food as good as mine, please continue behaving like you have done so far. Amit Ashar, Roshan Abbas, Kabir Khan, Yudishter Urs, Wendell Rodricks, Ajay Mago, Shakun Batra, Sanjay Chopra, Victor Acharya, Cyrus Sahukar, Gaurav Kapoor, Akshay Agarwal, Riteish Deshmukh, Kunal Khemu, Amit Sadh, Subash Kapoor, Samir Tiwari, Raj Jathar, Danny Hirji, Iqbal Warsi, Tosh Singh, Shyamal Vallabji, Soumik Sen, Mushtaq Sheikh, Vikram Sathaye, and Ankur Tiwari. Thank You.

Nikhil Chinnapa, for being part of my life, even if from afar.

Tosh Singh, you carried all my Le Creuset dishes for me from London. Only a really wonderful soul, who is also insane, would do something like that.

Mini Mathur, Jaya Mishra, Sandhya Mridul, Ritambhara Dewan, Sambo Parakh, Karishma Agarwal, Pooja Sawlani, Payal Singhal, Bhavna Ruparel, Bianca Louzado, Shaheen Abbas, Shruti Seth, Durrain Master, Tapur Chatterji, Banita Bikaji, Radhika Sawhney, Anusha Khan, Tisca Chopra, Kunika Singh, aunty Leela Khan and aunty Mridula Mishra for always encouraging me and being guinea pigs for most of the stuff I have cooked in these past years, and for sharing their recipes and always being there on rainy and sunny days.

Mini Mathur, for getting me the most amazing cook books and making me watch *Julie & Julia* which actually changed my life. For encouraging me every step of the way, for all the recipes you shared and continue to share, from your kitchen and your life.

Jaya Mishra, for making me start my food blog and for reading everything I wrote and giving me practical advice and believing in the insanity that makes it all work; for keeping me sane when I was going mad trying to get this book written and for keeping me open to all things possible in life.

Sandhya Mridul, for always believing that I would make it through cooking school, without running back home, and for pushing me to find the light you saw inside me.

Ritambhara Dewan, for being this silent strong force behind me, through all my ups and downs, for always being positive even if everything else was going crazy.

Sambo Parakh, for always being the zealous eater at the table and being part of this journey with me. Your time and effort were just invaluable, and your attention to detail, in your crazy Parsi way, was most lovable; thank you for believing in me.

Payal Singhal, for always being there and seeing to it that I looked very well turned out, every time it mattered and even when it didn't. I'm glad your beautiful clothes are part of this book.

Kichie, for never eating anything but the potatoes I make; because of you I learned to make them in a variety of ways, and thank you for always being on my side of the fence, regardless.

Bianca Louzado, for all the masalas you keep sending me, and the recipes attached, and for listening to me over the years and for so lovingly doing my make-up and hair for the cover of this book.

Shaheen Abbas, for sharing with me your tasty home recipes; for always being part of every feast I cook with full gusto; and for always giving me an unbiased opinion.

Priyanka Palkar, my make-up artist, for always making me look pretty in this book and otherwise.

Bhavna Ruparel, for being part of this book and for being the official taster, bounce light holder and the one who kept all our extras in order for the shoot.

Lorraine D'souza, my college friend, whose home I walked into nearly every weekend during my stint at Tante Marie, to eat East-Indian food and to just sleep. I don't think I would have gotten through those 11 weeks without you and your warm smile.

Sanjay and Rachna Narang, for just being so warm and always making me feel welcome in your home and heart. It's always a pleasure spending time with you, whether it is your home in India or in London, for making me part of your travel.

Junky and Pooja, I think coming to you to Budapest was an adventure that I will never forget. Pooja, for always bringing me ingredients I would not get back home, for always being the bringer of beautiful bake-ware and interesting recipes to try out.

Eve, my landlady in Woking. You made my stay so comfortable that it felt as if I was living with a close friend. We used to distribute the food I would get home from class, because you were a firm believer in 'sharing calories'.

Natasha Malhotra, my boss in MTV. I thank you for every fun and tough moment I spent at MTV; it made me the person I am. You believed that I was capable of far more than I thought I could do and thank you for bringing out in me all that and more.

Sneha Rajani, of Sony, you are one of the fairest persons I know. You gave me an opportunity to be part of the ICC Champions Trophy, 2002, and the Cricket World Cup, 2003, for believing I could be a travelling

host for cricket, knowing fully well I did not know as much as I needed to know, and I still don't.

Ajay Mago, for really believing in me when I really did not actually believe in myself; for having the patience and waiting for me, through building kitchens, going on holidays, moving homes, and laughing with me over kebabs on mountain tops.

Shoili Sarkar-Seth, my editor, and Ipshita Mitra, from Om Books International, for crossing my t's and dotting my i's, and for making a perfect sense of my ramblings.

Sucharita Suri, you were the oyster I was deep-sea diving for. Your design was just the perfect plate I was searching for, to present my food.

Vijay, my helper and my sous chef all rolled into one. You were a huge hands-on kitchen support during the making of this book, and were part of every experiment, disaster, shoot and reshoot that we did for this book. You are my team. Thank you Vijay Bhaiya.

Amit Ashar, I could not have done this without you and I knew that the only person who would be able to do justice to my food would be you. I thank you for your patience and I am utterly amazed at how you just bring every picture to life, and always find something humane in every little morsel that was cooked.

Now, for the ones who are a piece of my heart. A very big thank you to Zeke and Zene, the two little reasons that made me find a huge part of my life that I never knew existed. If it was not for the fact that you were the hungry little ones with voracious appetites, I may have never really pushed myself into my kitchen. The way you devour my food makes me feel like a Michelin Star chef and that is my biggest reward.

Finally, I'm going to save the last for the guy who never ever thinks of me as anything less than the best. Who may not agree with me, but never discourages me. Who never reads anything I write, but says 'I'm sure it's fantastic'. Who eats my food and thinks that I need to open a restaurant! Who cooked for me when he was free and buys me ingredients when he travels. Arshad Warsi, you are the king of the jungle, and I'm really happy to run around roaring with you.

P.S. IN CASE I HAVE FORGOTTEN TO THANK ANYONE, IT'S SINCERELY BLAMED UPON THE STARTING SYMPTOMS OF ALZHEIMER'S (TRUE STORY.... GRANDMA AGNES HAD IT), AND NOT FOR ANY LACK OF LOVE.

MY TEAM OF INCREDIBLES

AMIT ASHAR HE RATHER DEVOUR THE FOOD THAN SHOOT IT.
EVERY PLATE HE METICULOUSLY SHOT TESTED HIS WILL POWER.

SAMBO PARAKH SHE STYLES CLOTHES FOR FILMS. AND HERE SHE WAS
ARRANGING PLATES AND TABLES AND CONSTANTLY BARGAINING WITH ME
FOR MORE MEAT IN MY BOOK.

BHAVNA RUPAREL IN BETWEEN SHOOTING FOR FILMS AND ADS SHE
SLIPPED INTO THE ROLE OF REFLECTOR HOLDER AND CALM BRINGER.

VIJAY FROM MY MAN-FRIDAY TO SOUS CHEF, HE WAS MY ONE- POINT CONTACT FOR ALL
INGREDIENTS, LADLES AND VESSELS I EVER NEEDED TO MAKE THIS COOK BOOK WHAT IT IS.

AND PRESENTING...

OUR ABLE AND COMMITTED SUPPORT CAST

GLOSSARY

SOUPS (SP)

Creamy Prawn Spaghetti Soup pg 175
French Onion Soup pg 143
Grilled Tomato, Mushroom, Baby Corn Clear Soup pg 127
Mixed Vegetable Soup with Barley pg 95
Pak Choi, Tofu, Burnt Garlic, Egg Noodle Clear Soup pg 159
Palak Soup pg 15
Payaa Soup pg 111
Potato and Leek Soup pg 63
Roast Pumpkin Soup pg 31

SALADS (SL)

Avocado with Salsa pg 32
Baked Fig Salad pg 47
Baked Sweet Potato with Arugula Leaves pg 176
Beetroot Salad pg 16
Couscous Salad pg 112
Kale Salad pg 144
Micro Green Salad 160
Potato Salad with Dill pg 96
Roasted Pepper Salad pg 64
Watermelon and Feta Salad pg 128
Winter Salad pg 192

STARTERS (ST)

NON-VEGETARIAN

Chicken Honey Mustard Sausages pg 195
Chicken Liver on Papad pg 115
Mandeli Fry pg 51

VEGETARIAN

Asparagus Rolls with Hollandaise pg 34
Cheesy Choux Pastry pg 179
Cheesy Potato Skins pg 147
Khaari, Mozzarella and Caramelised Onion pg 131
Little Pizzettes pg 80
Onion in Red Wine and Melba Toast pg 48
Ragi Pancake with Mushrooms pg 18
Soya-Flavoured Edamame Beans pg 163
Sun-dried Tomato Hummus pg 99
Tomato, Onion and Basil Bruschetta pg 67

MAIN COURSE

NON-VEGETARIAN (MNV)

Baked Chicken pg 196
Basa in a Light Tomato Gravy pg 21
Bhutanese Lamb pg 164
Chicken Breast in Coconut Cream pg 148
Chicken Maple Syrup pg 100
Chicken Sausages with Pasta in a Cheesy Sauce pg 84
Clams in a Creamy Wine Sauce pg 68
Lamb Moile pg 52
Lamb Shank in Vindaloo Paste pg 132
Mini Lamb Burgers pg 83
Salmon with Crusted Pistachio pg 37
Salt-baked Fish pg 180
Slow-cooked Lamb Shanks or Lamb Kareli pg 116

VEGETARIAN (MV)

Baked Vegetables pg 183
Cauliflower Gratin pg 151
Cluster Beans (Guar) and Coconut pg 55
Grilled Zucchini Stuffed with Pasta Arrabiata pg 103
Mirchi Stuffed with Paneer Bhurji pg 119
Mushroom Risotto pg 38
Pancakes with Aubergine and Pepperonata Sauce pg 198
Pasta in a Cheesy Sauce with Green Peas pg 87
Stack of Aubergine with Yoghurt and Basil pg 135
Vegetable Momos pg 167
Vegetable Soufflé pg 70
Yellow Peppers Stuffed with Mixed
Vegetables and Quinoa pg 22

DESSERT (D)

Alphonso Meringue Madness pg 88
Bruschetta with Chocolate and Salt pg 136
Choco-Oozing Muffins pg 184
Coconut Pancakes pg 56
Khubani ka Meetha pg 120
Lemon Tart with Meringue pg 152
Mint-Flavoured Baked Yogurt pg 104
Orange Cake pg 73
Pear Poached in Rosé pg 25
Sticky Rice with Mango Pudding pg 168
Strawberry Hearts pg 41
Tiramisu pg 200

DRINK (DR)

Mulled Wine pg 191

NOTES

NOTES